Benjamin Casey

Solution of Bible Problems and Logic of the Scriptures

Benjamin Casey

Solution of Bible Problems and Logic of the Scriptures

ISBN/EAN: 9783337171940

Printed in Europe, USA, Canada, Australia, Japan

Cover: Foto ©Lupo / pixelio.de

More available books at **www.hansebooks.com**

SOLUTION OF BIBLE PROBLEMS

AND

Logic of the Scriptures;

OR

MARRIAGE OF THEOLOGY AND PHILOSOPHY.

Copyright, 1889, By Benjamin Casey.

ALL RIGHTS RESERVED.

IN THIRTEEN CHAPTERS,

TO WHICH IS ADDED A CRITICAL EXAMINATION OF ALL DISPUTED PARTS OF THE BIBLE, SHOWING THE PERFECT AGREEMENT OF THEOLOGY AND PHILOSOPHY IN ALL OF THE SCRIPTURE.

What, therefore, God hath joined together, let not man put asunder.—Matthew xix:6.

DES MOINES:
IOWA PRINTING COMPANY.
1890.

PREFACE.

Is there a logical solution shown for the mysteries of nature, by the church or the world, either with or without the Bible? For, those who do not acknowledge the bible, do not, cannot, show any solution of the mysteries of nature. And the orthodox world with the Bible in hand has accepted interpretations that show collisions and disputes, and inexplicable passages; and seems to assume that it is the strength and dignity of the Bible to be so high and so deep that the human intellect can never comprehend its vastness. But if the Bible does show clear logical reason, and harmony in itself, and in all nature with it, then those that have the Bible and profess to believe it, and still will concede the point that the Bible is dark and mysterious, such should search with becoming vigilance until the clearest solution is found for the existence of all things in nature, in the light of Bible teaching. But the very eminent minister of the cross will approach those passages that are called dark, and as if by immovable fate, they close the door of investigation against the human race. They say do not bring hypothesis on this sacred ground; we can only receive a "Thus saith the Lord when you presume to step on this undisputed ground for investigation." But divest the mind of prejudice and scrutinize closely any and all theology that does concede the charge of mystery and darkness in the Bible to be true; and it cannot be denied that all such theology rests on hypothesis, because there are many passages of the Bible correctly inserted in their theories, and these passages were selected according to the ideas of those who selected them. Again, those passages in the absence of other passages seem to contain the idea that the writer was trying to prove. But they do not furnish a "Thus saith the Lord" for the religious tenet they wish to establish, but on hypothesis, purely and only, they declare their theology proven by the scripture.

But in the following pages the object will be to show that the authorized version, or the King James translation of the Bible is perfectly clear, and without collision or self dispute, or mysteries or darkness, but is perfectly philosophical in all its parts, and we venture on hypothesis less than any theology we have seen or read. I could not expect to produce any treatise on such a subject without the use of some words or ideas that a reader might regard as being hypothetical. Neither do I expect to show even so small a volume, without many detectable mistakes. But I claim at the hand of every honest reader of these pages, that if you cannot condemn the ideas advanced, but are convinced that the object of the writer is reached, that you will not strike at it because of its imperfect. manner of appearance. But if you are a scholar, or a writer, or a thinker, come up to the help of the truth, and bring this subject out plain as noonday sun, and lift the Bible and its author out of the slander it has lain under so long before the world, and the church, also. And take from the infidels their weapon of power by which they have trampled down the Bible, and the truth, and the hope of the world, and the light of the world, and have by that very means held Christianity in the back ground; and turned millions of inquiring hearts away from the source and hope of life.

For the highness, the richness, the glory, and the splendor can be seen only when the Bible is clearly understood, without mystery or darkness, or appearance of self contradiction. THE AUTHOR.

INTRODUCTION.

The stronghold of infidelity against the Bible, and against Christianity is that they charge the whole revelation with lack of reason, logic, philosophy and harmony within itself:

1. They say there is no trustworthy evidence of a God only in the Bible, and that they dispute. But that is treated in chapter 1, first part.

2. They say that the doctrine of the atonement is perfectly insupportable, being neither philosophical, nor logical, nor reasonable, and is a violation of justice and truth, love and mercy. The atonement is treated in the first chapter.

3. They say that geological testimony proves the bible account of creation to be untrue. But creation is treated in chapter 2 of this writing, and in chapter 3 on formation.

4. They say the origin of sin involves unsolvable difficulty, and the church does not meet them on that. But that is treated in chapter 4.

5. Fall of angels and men is not reconcilable with the perfect character that is ascribed to the God of the Bible. But see chapter 5 of this writing.

6 They say that if a God of infinite power and

wisdom did create this earth, and does over-rule all its inhabitants, then he must be the author of all that is done by all his creatures, and is responsible for all the consequences of sin, and misery, and death, both temporal and eternal. But see warfare in chapter 6, and also treated in chapters 4 and 5.

7. Types of the old testament. They say that the flood, and the universal destruction in wars of human life is not in harmony with infinite goodness But these were necessities in nature and are treated of in chapter 7.

8. They say that the doctrine of human salvation by faith is wholly insupportable and is the sacrifice of justice and truth. But see chapter 8.

9. They say the Bible doctrine of future reward and punishment is the sacrifice of justice and truth, love and mercy. But see chapter 9 on the philosophical necessity of the doctrines, based on cause and effect.

10. They say there is no evidence of the divine authenticity of the scriptures, neither that it is the genuine work, as was first given to the world. This is treated in chapter 11.

Chapter 10 treats of the possible design of revelation. Chapter 12 treats of the translation of A. D. 1611. These are the main points on which the infidel holds the appearance of success against the Bible. But out of them grows multitudes of objections of much smaller consequence and inferior importance.

And they boldly and defiantly challenge the world and the church to show reason or logic on these special points, and if these ten or twelve main points of Bible teaching cannot be shown to be logically reasonable by the church, and the advocates of the Bible, then it is claimed that whatever grows out of these leading passages has as strong claim to truth as the leading passages they grow out of.

They further say that the most profound critics, and thinkers, and writers all agree that the best interpretations of the scriptures do involve these collisions, these irreconcilable passages, and that it is impossible to show reason in them, either with or without the aid of the Bible, or by any possible argument that can be brought, none can show logical truth in the Bible at these points of apparent contradiction. And the minister that finds more interest in the sumptuous feast, with the sprightly company than he finds in searching out the depths of the word of life, these are apt to say "Do not bring any argument in defense, of such a cause, except it is supported by a 'Thus saith the Lord.'" So then argument is barred by the Christians and defied by the infidel.

But if there is argument brought, either from revelation or from nature, or from both, that will show these several topics to be in harmony with themselves and with all nature, then the infidel is answered. But if another interpretation of the Bible is shown that is based on the clearest philosophy, but holds the entire scripture in perfect harmony, and that it is true on the ground of natural necessity, and clears up every objection that was ever, or can ever be brought against the Bible, then the objecting Christian should feel answered, and the Bible should be regarded a philosophical book.

The object of this writing is to defend all parts of the scripture in the light of the clearest philosophy, without dispute or difficulty in any part of it.

B. C.

CHAPTER I.

PHILOSOPHY DEMONSTRATES THE GOD OF THE BIBLE BY THE LAWS OF NATURE.—HIS ATTRIBUTES SECURITY FOR ALL CREATED THINGS.—NECESSITY FOR ATTONEMENT BEFORE CREATION.—TESTIMONY NATURAL AND SCRIPTURAL.

In order to show a logical solution of the mysteries of nature there must be information brought from some source beyond nature itself, for it is clear that nature alone does not solve the mystery.

But can the book of Revelation show philosophical reason for all things in clear harmony with all nature? Can the God of the Bible be demonstrated by the testimony of nature, independent of the Bible? If it can be so done, then the Bible may be considered reliable. Now, when we see many things in nature which are absolutely necessary to human life, as well as all animal life, which are not produced by visible power, but design meets necessity perfectly, that proves a designer. And if the learning and talent of man utterly fail to show the first principles of such design, or its origin; when it is further shown that the Bible account is in perfect harmony with all nature, and will clear up all mysteries in nature, then the God of the Bible is demonstrated in the light of the clearest philosophy. But if it is said that the mysteries of nature are produced, or brought about by the laws of nature, the answer is that such is the design of the laws of nature to govern the material world. And it is so filled with natural and intelligent design that so perfectly meets natural necessity that it is impossible for honest inquiry to fail to see the indisputable evidence of a designer. And when very many things are seen that are not necessary to life, but of great convenience, in which design and necessity meet perfectly, the evidence of a designer is still more abundant. And when all nature, apart from Revelation, utterly fails to find the origin of these designs, and there cannot be an effect without a cause, then can philosophy be stronger, or more perfectly clear in anything than is shown for the God of the Bible? Hence the absurdity of the idea that the laws of nature exist without a designer; and effects so filled with design exist without a cause, or intelligent designer, although men of great power of mind have adopted those ideas, and no marvel, because such do not make the subject their study. But when the objection is overcome in the hands of great men, then the truth will be indisputably proven.

If the great of the earth did not defend the wrong, then the wrong could not be perfectly overcome and the world would fail of its mission. But the wrong must be overcome in the hands of the strongest men that choose to take hold of it.

But notice some of the evidences that nature bears to the existence of the God of the Bible, in such things as are necessary to life, and their perfect fitness to supply the demands, and their comforts and bliss to animal life, and wherein necessity, intelligence and design are fully developed in the same thing. Think of the folly of doubting a designer?

1. The breath of life, or atmosphere. Deprive animal life of air, and one hour would extinguish all animal life. But man is a necessity in nature very far beyond anything that is in himself, and the intelligent design of air for his support is perfect, and for the support of all animal life for man's sake directly and indirectly.

2. Water. All animal life must perish of thirst if water could not be obtained. But how it abounds in the earth, and no man can estimate its value as a comfort, a blessing.

3. Food. Who can produce food, even if the world were perishing for want of it? Not one, save the Almighty only, and yet men live.

4. Fire. How necessary to life, and vastly more so for comfort and convenience. Man can produce the fire if he has the material, but fire, as a principle in nature, belongs to the Divine only.

5. Rain-fall to make the earth produce. Life depends on rain-fall as really as on breath. But that also belongs to the Divine only.

6. Growth of animals and vegetables without which life must soon become extinguished. But the laws of growth are with the Almighty only.

7. Sleep, as necessary to life as food or drink. But it is of the Lord.

8. The power of sight.

9. The power to hear.

10. The law of life, vegetable or animal.

None of these can be accounted for only as they are solved in the God of the Bible; but the Bible is the most logically reasonable solution of all the mysteries of nature that can be given for anything.

But beside all these there is much more that enters into the necessities of life.

11. For if life is sustained it is by power of motion which is a separate gift.

12. Intelligence, or power of thought, separate.

13. Law of attraction on which not only animal life depends, but also the existence of the planets. Tide or ebb and flow of the sea. The rain-fall is in the right direction. The magnet attracts the needle.

But to mention a few more without comment.

14. Electricity ought to be classed with the others.

15. Steam.

16. Nitroglycerine, and all manner of poisons and very much more powder, and all explosives.

And when these are all considered there still remains a question in everything in nature, that the eye beholds, which cannot be answered only as the Bible finds the answer. All bear testimony to the God of the Bible. Now, in the nature of things, it is impossible to prove anything so strong as the testimony of nature proves the existence of the God of the Bible, and that evidence establishes the fact that the Bible account of him is true.

And although these topics are all familiar and are the topics of common conversation, yet when they are brought into such connection as this, who can turn its force aside, seeing it is logical? And more especially, when the philosopher has sought so long in vain to find a reasonable solution of nature's mysteries apart from the Bible. Philosophy brings cause and effect for the explanation of nature. All good. All possible argument from cause and effect will establish the Bible if the argument finds its right place. But the very law of cause and effect, the boasted weapon of infidelity, will utterly destroy its cause, seeing that cause and effect cannot reach to the bottom of anything in nature independent of the Bible.

Do not these arguments demonstrate the God of the Bible from the book of nature alone, independently of the Bible? And when the God of the Bible is proven by the immovable testimony that nature alone furnishes, independently of the Bible, then is the Bible His word and His work, and then is the Bible itself the philosophical demonstration that it is of divine origin. Then the entire translation of 1611 is seen to be right just as it is, nothing added, nothing diminished.

And here let two propositions be laid down, never to be moved, and nothing admitted into theology that is not in the clearest harmony with both. The first one is the God of the Bible cannot do wrong, nor do evil, nor in any way cause them to be done, but can and does overrule them. The second one is that the origin of all evil, and all wrong is a self existent principle in nature that is the opposite of, the antagonist of all that enters into the divine character, and is the enemy of the universe. Hence, the intelligent agent is not the origin of sin, but he is the willing dupe of the great monster, Wrong, a principle in nature not a person. Herein is the reason why there is a wicked world, because in it is the vast warfare in which this enemy of universal nature must be overcome in all its bearings. This planet exists expressly for that purpose, and the war must go on until that work is completed. All the human race do choose their army to fight in, and all must abide the consequence of their choice. Then why is a miracle not as logical when done by divine authority as if a strong man would perform an act that his little child could not perform? The Bible must be successfully disproved before it is rational to deny the logic of a miracle that is attributed to the Almighty.

This whole subject must be considered in the light of the Bible only, but not in the light of popular theology, and no hypothesis admitted that will not show the most infinite perfection in the divine character, in all its attributes. For righteousness and justice require that when rational, intelligent agents are created who are capacitated to suffer or to enjoy, that the power that created them should provide ample security for their reasonable chance to attain to a state of bliss and happiness. This security is found in the perfection of the divine attributes, of which there are in Scripture seven spoken of each one independent of itself, the seven spirits of God, so called in Rev., 1: iv, and 3: i, and 4: v, and 5: vi. These were typified by the seven lamps always burning in the tabernacle day and night. The lamps burn before the throne. They are sent forth into all the earth. These seven attributes, or eternal principles in nature, and spirits of God are the foundation, the security of all things that are created, whether planet or agent. They are the security of all life, whether angels or men. Hence, in the construction of any theological basis, these seven spirits, these seven lamps, these seven essential attributes, must be maintained in their infinite perfection. To mar one of these attributes would sacrifice God head. It would undeify self-existent Deity, and there could be no perfection remaining in the universe. And as the fact is plain that nothing less than perfect purity, and infinity dwelling in every attribute, can create, then to render one of these imperfect would have been essentially to bar creation everlastingly. So let nothing be admitted into theology that will not leave these attributes perfectly clear. These seven are Truth, Love, Power, Wisdom, Justice, Mercy and Immutability. These are productive of all righteousness and all good, but cannot produce wrong or evils, though they have power to restrain and control any and all evil and all wrong. But what relation does the atonement sustain to these attributes? For the scripture shows that the atonement was foreordained before the foundation of the world. I Peter, 1: xx. And in still stronger terms in Mi., 5: ii—"He should come forth out of Bethlehem that should be ruler in Israel whose goings forth have been from of old, from everlasting." And Eph., 3: xi says: "According to the eternal purpose which he purposed in Christ Jesus, our Lord." These two passages put the atoner and his work back to the everlasting and to the eternal. Col., 1: xv, xvi, xvii, says: "All things were created by Him, and He is before all things, and by Him all things consist." The atonement was in force as far back as the name of the Atoner is found, and the atonement was virtually as effective when it was decreed by divine authority as it is to-day. It was in full force in all its bearings before creation did or could commence. Then, and not till then, could the Atoner create planets and agents.

But why would, or how could, Goodness and Righteousness decree that His beloved and only son should fill the place that He did fill in this world to atone for sin when there was not a sin, nor a sinner, in existence?

This is the difficulty that bothers the world, and the church, and holds the Bible in such indefensible weakness.

But if these spirits of God are each of them a virtue, then of necessity each one must have its opposite in principle, which, when developed, is a vice; otherwise there could be no virtue. But the opposite of truth is falsehood; of love is malice; of power is weakness; of wisdom is ignorance; of justice is injustice or wrong; of mercy is cruelty; and of immutability is vacillation. These were the natural antagonists of the divine character, but only as principles in nature, and could not be developed until some created agents would exist that they could act upon. But Wisdom saw this enemy, this antagonistic principle in nature, like the principle of fire that is not developed, but the principle is everywhere. One is a good figure of the other. And Wisdom saw the enemy ready to assail anything that could be created, and his own perfect nature made it impossible to create agents and expose them to that enemy until that enemy was brought under control, and its power virtually annihilated.

Here impossibilities seemed to meet, for the enemy could not be overcome without creature agents, and creature agents could not be exposed to that enemy's contamination until the power of that enemy was brought under divine control to the extent that the agents could, if they would, resist the tempter. This condition of things left but one possibility in nature, and that was that self-existent Deity should go in debt for all the expenses of a war sufficiently vast to overcome this enemy, and bring its power to a close forever. Hence, the divine decree that a body should be prepared for Him to wear to make atonement for sin, and a race of beings prepared for soldiers, and suffered to be fallen passively, but all redeemed, and that mercy should be offered to all alike, and that with the end of this world the work of the enemy should be destroyed forever, and the enemy and all his servants should be confined to a safe prison limit everlastingly.

Now, put those seven virtues together and treat

them under the head, or word, Right, and also consider the seven vices together and call them Wrong, narrowing the question down to a single word for each side, namely, Right and Wrong. For these seven all enter into the principle of wrong.

Now, if the wrong was as accessible as the right and as readily reached from any place that a spirit or a physical being could occupy, then that was the enemy, and it is from everlasting. Hence, the atonement must measure back with the occasion that required it.

Th s view of the atonement relieves it of all the difficulty that had previously gathered around it, and shows it to be an absolute necessity in nature and to occupy just the place and period that it does in the Lord's rulings and workings in the universe in the light of Bible teaching. But the commonly received opinion is that the atonement was ordained after the fall of man seemed to require it; such opinion must plunge the whole subject into unfathomable and hopeless difficulty. For if man was created very good, and if the fallen spirits were also created very good; but if some of them did originate sin and thus fell, then the power that originated those that are fallen is the cause of all the consequences of the fall, and becomes the author of all sin, and also the cause of all suffering and death; thus all the lost of this earth and all the lost spirits will charge their loss and their suffering to the creator; all of the seven attributes are sacrificed, and the Bible cannot be regarded as a book of truth.

But if the great adversary of the creator and of all righteousness and all happiness and bliss, and the originator of wrong and sin and suffering and death —temporal and spiritual, was an uncreated principle in nature, eternal as Deity, but was like the principle of fire, it cannot be developed without fuel; but if suitable fuel is prepared, and the match lighted, fire is developed. Very like that was the principle of wrong. It could not be developed until created beings could be reached. But when there were created agents in existence, both spiritual and physical, then the principle was soon developed, and the ordaining of the atonement was the declaration of war; "for the invisible things of Him are clearly seen, being understood by the things that are made, so that they are without excuse."—Rom. 1:20. We cannot plead ignorance in so plain a case.

But when the fullness of period arrived to bring the war into active operation, then the world, the ground of action, is here, and the human race for the soldiers; and all was very good, for the Lord couldn't bring into existence anything that was not very good; the armed soldiers with a weapon that could defend them everlastingly if they would use it faithfully; but if they listened to the tempter, and sinned and fell, and all the race with and in them, so that the enemy was permitted to gain a victory over the entire race of man; and the strong man, armed, would fain keep his palace and his goods in peace, but the stronger came on him and took the soldiers of the cross from his ranks and drilled and disciplined them for four thousand years, then the commander came to the field of action in person, and the hand to hand fight commenced when the two champions met in the temptation in the wilderness, and it was manifest that the strong man could not hold the palace. Though the commander has gone to live in the Capitol, yet he still commands his army, and must, and will, until these seven spirits of God have gained a perfect victory over the enemy in all its possible bearings.

Truth must overcome falsehood, and power must overcome weakness, and wisdom overcome ignorance, and love must overcome malice, and justice overcome injustice, and mercy overcome cruelty, and immutability overcome vascillation; or, to use the two words, right must overcome wrong; and men are invited up to so highly a dignified relation as to take a part in this vast warfare of eternal consequences. Spiritual weapons must overcome carnal weapons.

CHAPTER II.

THE WORK OF CREATION.

Creation could not proceed until the work of atonement was ratified and made reliable. But it is said, "In the beginning God created the heaven and the earth." The word "create" here is often explained by the legislative powers of the world. The legislature of a state often creates a new county by passing and confirming an act that a new county shall be formed from parts of several other counties that exist when the act is passed. But the new county is without form and void like the earth was when it was created. But when the old county officers' term of office expires and the counties, new and old, elect their officers, and they are duly qualified and the new county organized and platted, then it is formed and then it is not without form, nor void. But it exists as a new and a real county as any other in the state, a ready figure of the first chapter of Genesis. All things in nature were created, but were without form and void, until the proper period would arrive for any thing to be useful, then it would be formed and become useful. But in the second chapter it treats of the formation of all vegetables, and animals, of the earth, but not of the earth itself. Neither is it said at what period the earth was formed. But it was found ready for man when man was formed. If the geologist wants to go back any number of years the Bible is not in his road. But more of that under the head of "Formation."

But consider the vastness of the work of creation, all planets, and worlds, and the devising, and determining the orbit in which every one should move, and the place in the vastness of space that everyone should occupy, the relative distance of each, from all others, and the laws by which all should be governed in their respective orbits and all laws needful to rule any planet, in any way would be, or was created with the planet, in a connection so inseparable, that when any planet would be required and called for, or formed it would come forth with every nature perfect that is needful for it. Just like any animal or vegetable. When a man comes into being he brings all the faculties of a man with him. All was provided for in creation. And so with every planet that ever did, does now, or ever will exist. But they may not all be formed yet, maybe not the half of them, though all were created in the beginning. But the planet on which we live presents to us more interest than all the others at this time and we have a much more minute description of its creation than all the others. One reason for that is because we could not understand an account of the others if the laws, manners, and habits are different from our own. Another reason is we have no need of such knowledge. But the essential reason why we are instructed more minutely on the creation of this planet than any of the others, is because there are so many unmistakable testimonies that this is the most important planet that the Lord has use for, or that is in nature. But why? Because it is a fallen planet? may be asked. Yes, and in the nature of things Justice required its redemption, and an atonement for sin. And in connection with redemption and atonement for sin also the entire overthrow of every principle of wrong, with all the fruit it bears, and the utter destruction of its power ever to produce insurrection in the Lord's kingdom again or to tempt his weakest servant. All this was embraced in the creation of this planet, and on it that entire work must be finished and yet a great amount more. For on this planet the Lord should make a revelation of himself to all his subjects, a revelation whose words should never pass away, for the revelation the Lord makes was made in wisdom, for necessary purposes, and its necessity can never cease. But this planet was created with perfect adaptedness for instrumentalities that by, and in it, the Lord would make his revelation perfect.

And yet another necessary, and vastly great design in the creation of this planet was for a theater of war, and that, short-sighted man can see. Just open the eyes and see, and admire the perfect adaptedness of this entire earth to, and for that vast purpose. A very great part of this is revealed to man by his physical senses and is not, nor need not be, a matter of written revelation; for in either case, the instruction is of the Lord, and does make men responsible for what knowledge they have: whether by written or natural revelation.

But every intelligent mind sees, and cannot evade the force of the facts as they are seen, that constant conflict is going on in the world, of right against wrong, wisdom against folly, and love against malice. Every possible thing that is not right is the enemy of right, and the concentrated powers of every species, character, or magnitude of them join their powers to gain victory over the right, and the human agents are put on their responsibility. The Lord says, " occupy till I come." Here is wrong with its wages, and also here is right with its gifts and rewards: Choose and act. But settle every one his own account when it is full.

But exceedingly more than all this is embraced or comprised in the creation of this planet, and its adaptedness for the accomplishment of the vast purpose for which it was designed. This requires all needful instrumentalities to do the work. Leading spirits of superior power and skill in the physical world would choose the cause of wrong, and act as its champions with all the physical and mental power they possess that there would be so many of that class in every age of the world that the cause of wrong and its champions would bear endless testimony that carnal weapons could not prevail over spiritual weapons though they seemed to possess all possible advantage and hold it for a long time.

But in creation; this planet should possess an adaptness for other important necessities for this vastly important warfare. In the nature of things the enemy could not be conquered if it would not be brought into close conflict with the power that could conquer it; hence the necessity for these champions of wrong, and so many of them, and of such vast power and skill, so that wrong in all its forms and magnitudes is brought into conflict with the Author of right, and the soldier of the cross, and the spiritual weapons of the spiritual warfare to meet their utter and endless overthrow.

But it may be thought and said, that the Scripture teaches that it is the Lord's love and mercy toward man that moves him to such displays of kindness toward the human race, and not for some vastly greater design that lies far back of, and beyond the interests of the human race. But say, O, man, if all that is written in the scriptures of the Lord's goodness to man is true and a very great amount more, (for so it is), does it make the mercies any less valuable; because there was real necessity for the whole race outside of themselves that was the essential reason for their existence ? And are the mercies and blessings and high privileges not as worthy of the homage of the heart, of the fidelity, loyalty, the worship and the praise, (could I say more?) of all the earth as if no other object had been in the divine purpose but the interest of man? But to look at this world as we see it; and say that there was no object in its existence higher than is seen in its self, is weakness in the eyes of either Christian or infidel. But if we see the soldiers of the cross struggling in the war, dying at their posts, conquerers of the world, and afterward exalted to a triumphant relation with their commander of the army that conquered the enemy of the universe, and exhibited in that relation forever, then there is seen philosophy in this world.

There are those who are still of the opinion that the first chapter of Genesis means formation as well as creation, but do not explain the difficulties that it involves therein. For example, " the earth was without form and void," and the third day shows the growing of trees and grass. But the fourth day shows the creation of sun, moon and stars, involving natural impossibilities, and yet some think the infidel should not show the absurdity of such an opinion! And again in the creation man and woman are brought to view at the same time; and the last of all things created. Impossible to reconcile it with the second chapter, which shows man first of all, then the vegetables and animals of earth, then the woman. But if we take the first chapter for creation or legislation, and the second chapter for formation, both are clear and right, for the plants and herbs of the field were created in the first chapter. But in second chapter, at the formation, the plants had not been in the earth, nor had not grown, nor had there been rain upon the earth, and there was not a man to till the ground. But then formation goes on.

Other thoughts are noticed in other pages, but notice one more here. That is, it is said to be 4004 years from the commencement of the life of the first man Adam to the birth of our Savior, and we are in the 1887th year of the christian era. These two periods added make 5891 years. But it is said that in the beginning God created the heaven and the earth. Such an opinion seems to place the beginning or the commencement of creation 5891 years ago. Now if the Creator is without beginning, can wisdom be found in such an idea? And the ideas that have been held that creation and formation mean the same thing are contrary to the scriptures and to reason, and shut the truth out from the Bible, and throw impenetrable darkness over that part of the scripture. But in the light of these pages, all is plain scriptural, philosophical and easily seen.

CHAPTER III.

ON FORMATION.

Formation is the act of bringing anything into existence, but creation is the legislative authority that anything and everything shall be brought into existence when wisdom requires them, but nothing sooner. All things in nature were created within a period that the Bible terms six days; and a seventh day was a day of rest; and after this or then, we might suppose Him that rested was refreshed, but no part of creation had yet appeared. Every possible thing in nature was endowed in its creation with every qualification that could be necessary to make it perfect, to answer the design for which it was intended; so that when anything would be formed, whether planet or person, men or angels, all would come into being perfectly fitted to fill their places. Hence the Lord said, at the close of creation, " Behold it is all very good." —Genesis 1:31.

The second chapter of Genesis very briefly treats of formation, but not of creation, except the first three verses that belong to the first chapter. The earth is formed here ready for man when man was formed, but no account of when the earth was formed. Other scripture informs us that other planets were in existence before ours, or this earth. Job, xxxviii:4-7.

The Lord said to Job: "Where was thou when I laid the foundations of the earth? declare, if thou hast understanding. Who hath laid the measures thereof, if thou knowest? or who hath stretched the line upon it? whereupon are the foundations thereof fastened? or who laid the corner stone thereof, when the morning stars sang together, and all the sons of God shouted for joy?" This shows, for the scriptures cannot be broken, that when the first move was made to form this earth that there were stars to sing, and there were sons to shout. That meets all the difficulty in the first chapter, about the growth of vegetation before the sun gave light or heat. It also removes all opposition from the science of geology, for if the geologist wants to make the period millions of ages since the earth was formed, the Bible is not in the road. It shows that all the planets were not formed at one time, or period; and they may not all be in existence yet; for although all were created in the beginning; nothing should be formed until wisdom required it, then Omnipotence would call it, and it would come forth in all perfection. But to return to the formation of the animal and vegetable departments of this earth; begin with the fourth verse: "These are generations of the heavens and of the earth when they were created, in the day that the Lord God made the earth and the heavens;" fifth verse: "And every plant of the field before it was in the earth, and every herb of the field before it grew; for the Lord God had not caused it to rain upon the earth, and there was not a man to till the ground."

In the fifth verse it says the plants and herbs were created and made, but had not been in the earth, nor had ever grown, nor had there ever been rain upon the earth, nor was there a man to till the ground. The plants, and herbs, and the rain, and man had been created, but had not been formed. Surely, how could it ever have been misunderstood or seem dark to any one?

But the sixth verse gives account of the first rain, and the seventh verse gives an account of the formation of the entire human race in the person of the first man—"And man became a living soul," the entire race of man, including the body that our Lord lived in, what was earthly of it. Of the dust of the ground the Lord God formed man, and out of the ground made the Lord God to grow all vegetation; and out of the ground the Lord God formed every beast of the field, and every fowl of the air. In all this forming the word "create" is not used. But when the woman appeared another word was used: "And the rib which the Lord God had taken from the man, made He a woman and brought her to the man." She was formed in the person of a man; but when she was transformed, it is described by the words "made He a woman."

Surely these remarks on formation must demonstrate that formation and creation are entirely different, having but little analogy thé one to the other. When the Lord created man in His own likeness, in the image of God created He him, male and female created He them. But nothing more about them till formation is spoken of, and then we read, "And the Lord God formed man of the dust of the ground, and breathed into his nostrils the breath of life, and man became a living soul." Here was the physical and the spiritual man. But after man was formed; he is, and is a living soul; and after beasts and fowls were formed they were living, active creatures, like the man; for we see them all pass before the man to receive their name. After all this, the woman was brought to view, but she was not formed, for she was formed in the person of Adam. But a rib was taken from Adam or the man, "made He a woman," and brought her to the man. So different are the accounts of the creation and formation that it is the weakness of the Bible's claim to truth to try to reconcile the two chapters to mean the same thing. But if the first chapter means creation or legislation, and the second chapter means formation or execution, then both are perfectly clear, and all trouble is removed out of the way of philosophy and also out of the way of geology.

In these chapters the principles of theology and philosophy meet and are perfectly reconciled to each other. The proper interpretation of the scripture is the proper theology, and in every particular proper theology and true philosophy are at perfect agreement. If there were a large money reward offered for showing clear philosophy to be in perfect harmony with clear theology, it would soon be done. But why should it not be the object of everybody's search until it is found? Is this very thing not the cause of the distraction of all civilized countries? England and Germany and the United States, are all taxing their learning and their eminent scholars to find reconciliation between theology and philosophy. But it is sought in the wisdom of the world, and its plain simplicity overlooked.

Why should it be unpardonable heresy to dissent from Martin Luther, or John Calvin, or George Fox, the Quaker, or John Wesley? These were all great reformers and brought very much light on questions that most needed to be made clear, in their day. But other questions have arisen since their day that, at this time, need to be shown up in a light that will show reason, power and clearness in the Bible, and rescue the Bible and Christianity from under the feet of infidelity, and enable all Christians to see that they have a philosophically permanent foundation for the hope that is within them.

I wish to bring one more idea on the relation that formation sustains to creation. That is in the person of Jesus Christ, who was so connected with the Divine that he was counted the foundation of all things, head of all things; the bed-rock of all creation, and was an absolute necessity for the existence of all things; or of anything at all, and He was created or ordained before creation commenced. This is clear from the fact that all things were created by Him. His physical body was formed in the person of the first man, Adam, but this person of so vast importance to all nature, was not produced until 4004 years after Adam's life commenced. Now the philosophy of all this is the infinity of all the attributes that make up the Divine character, for His purposes are all devised in infinite wisdom, and His infinite power secures the certainty of His purposes, as really when the purpose is determined as it can be after the work is performed, like the acts, or decrees, of a responsible government.

But if the very greatest events in nature are ordained first of all, yet their development deferred through vast periods utterly unknown to flesh and blood, or human mind, then is it unreasonable to admit the idea that this planet and the human race were created in the beginning, but not formed until wisdom required them, and the period for them to be useful had arrived? Here we see that theology and philosophy meet and marry together and live in the oneness of that relation perfectly. But satan and his servants try to sever them. "What God hath joined together let not man put asunder." But how successful has the enemy been in sundering this marriage in the eyes of the church and of all the world. This principle is also seen in nature around us, for how many instances have been developed, of a man and a woman joining their destinies in marriage, lawful and honorable, but a fascinating man marks that young wife for his victim. Or a woman of similar fascinating power will mark the young husband for her victim, and they will meet the object of their fiendish hope, anywhere, at church, or at their home, or on the street, in the store, or any place, and often meet by appointment, until the lawful marriage is hopelessly severed, or the parties cease to love ever after. Now the severing of the marriage relation that God hath ordained in either of the instances is the work of that enemy that the Lord and His servants are conquering in the great warfare of the earth. But what estimate can be set on the man or the woman that will become the willing dupe in the hand of the devil to do that contemptible work that a fallen spirit could not do in person? An old Christian man said in my presence, speaking in love feast, as he stood near the pulpit, that some men were meaner than the devil, for the devil could not do every low, mean, dirty thing, but he could send some man to do it for him, at the same time putting his hand on his preacher's knee with a gentle shake, greatly to the mirth of the audience. And if the old man's estimation is possible, that a man or woman can get down lower and meaner than the devil, it is found in the person that will sever the marriage relation.

CHAPTER IV.

ORIGIN OF SIN.

First—Who could not be, nor was not the author of sin.

Second—What was, and in the nature of things, must be the author of sin.

How, or by whom could sin have been originated, or can that be seen both logically and scripturally?

The Creator could not originate sin or wrong, nor could He create any being that could originate sin or wrong, because He is infinitely good and He is infinite in every attribute of goodness, and is not capable of doing wrong or evil, or in any way causing them to be done. If he would create an agent whether spirit or physical agent that could and would originate sin or wrong that would make Him the origin of all sin. Thus the fountain and source of all goodness would be found to be the author of all sin and wrong, and of all their consequences, all suffering and death in the physical world, and also of the everlasting punishment in the world of lost spirits. This must be true, because Wisdom knew the end from the beginning, and could not but know all the consequences of the acts of any creature to whom He would give up life and intelligence to choose; therefore, to produce such agent, knowing the consequences of such production, must make the producer the author of all the agent does.

Such authorship in the Creator would be the sacrifice of every attribute of the divine character.

If sin was not the product of a self-existent principle in nature co-eternal with the Almighty, and ndependent of Him, then all things in nature must exist by the Creator's power and authority. Hence, it would be in the nature of things impossible to exonerate the Creator from the authorship of all the sin and suffering in the universe.

And yet another reason why the great enemy of the universe was a self-existent principle in nature, and that all choosing a sinful life are but the servants of that enemy is found in the fact that it is impossible for infinite purity and perfection to do wrong. Consequently, if there had not been some principle in nature that was the source of evil and sin and wrong, and not subject to the divine command, then if the Lord of the universe did not originate the sin, and creatures could not, sin nor wrong could never have been seen, and all creation would be one vast heaven of bliss and happiness.

An infidel, in his argument against the Bible, said that right and wrong are eternal, and evidently thought it an unanswerable argument against the Bible. But this is the very dagger that will shed the blood of infidelity without mercy. For wrong, being an eternal principle in nature, not created, but self-existent, it is the first cause and the essential element of all evil, and is itself the origin of sin. The first element of wrong is possibility, and possibility is the first essential element in the existence of anything. Many possibilities are unknown to the human race for ages because they are not developed. But when some mind is led to see the possibility, and to search out the means for its development, and bring the possibility to view or into existence. Then it is developed, but possibility underlies every other condition of its existence, like unto the power of electricity, as in the telegraph, the electric light, or any other use to which it is put. But if it is claimed that origin implies action, then the first action taken is the origin of any work, but the origin of the nature or principle of any work, whether good or evil, is found in the natural principle of the work produced. Good cannot be evil, and neither can evil be good.

The sin or evil that becomes visible is the fruit that the principle bears, but it is developed by the agent that produces it, the principle itself being the origin of its fruit.

Here is the true solution of the origin of sin, which removes all the difficulty from that vast question that ever gathered round it, and is in harmony with all the Scripture, and with all things in nature. It is the only answer to the great question that has taxed the learning and the talent of the principal countries of the globe, Germany, France, England and America. This explanation of the origin of sin, together with one more thought as prominent and as troublesome as itself, will remove almost all difficulties from the Bible. That thought is that this planet was called into existence expressly for the purpose of a warfare for the overthrow of that vast enemy of all righteousness, and peace, and happiness and comfort and enjoyment—the origin of sin.

These two great truths when seen in their reasonable and scriptural light, will show why the wickedness of this world is suffered by an overruling power of infinite goodness, because it is the only possible way to overcome the monster, and like some wars of the world, the objects or benefits are so vast it will justify the expense it costs.

The idea that sin was originated by some created agent of vast intelligence must necessarily leave the entire charge of wrong, with all its unfathomable consequences, on the Creator. All sin of all worlds, and all the fruit that wrong and sin bear, which is death spiritual and physical; all suffering, whether physical or spiritual, as well as the everlasting punishment in the world of hopeless despair; all that descends from such agent must as a matter of necessity descend from the power that endowed that agent with power to originate the wrong, or the sin, and to perpetuate it. But we see the origin of sin was a principle in nature that was without origin, but was self-existing, as was the principle of right, and for which the Creator was not responsible, but is like the principle of fire in the material world, which cannot be seen until the necessary agent, fuel, is produced, and caused to ignite; then fire is developed.

The fire is a clear figure of the great principle of wrong existing in nature co-eternal with the principle of right, which could not be developed until intelligent agents were created. But agency implies the power of choice, and when created agents came into existence they could not exist out of reach of right and wrong, the one as easy of access as the other. The principle of right was the origin of all good, and the principle of wrong was the origin of all evil, or sin. But self-existent

Deity contained the principle of all righteousness, and made provision to meet the self-existent enemy that existed in nature before the creation of anything could or did commence. For the name of Jesus Christ is brought to our understanding from everlasting, and from the eternal, and as far back as that name appears as connected with the ruling of the human race, so far back was all His work appointed to Him, leaving men without excuse if they cannot defend His word on the principles of the clearest logic and the most philosophical reason.

For it is a natural impossibility for the Creator, who is perfect and pure, to create agents with faculties really necessary for agency, and put them any place in boundless space, where the wrong would not be as accessible to them as the right. But the wrong could not be developed until created agents would exist for the wrong to act upon.

CHAPTER V.

FALL OF ANGELS AND MEN.

By what, or by whom, was the fall produced? The Lord could not produce it and creatures could not, but a principle, not a person, could. At the close of the narrative of creation, it is written that God saw everything that he had made, and beheld that it was very good. But after this, the human race was formed in the person of the first man, and a part of the man was transformed into a woman, and in them was the rite of marriage established. The next account we have of them was that they were tempted, and sinned, and fell, and were no more very good. Whence came the temptation? The Bible reads thus, "The serpent beguiled the woman." But in latter days it is said the devil tempted the woman. Was he always a devil? It is mostly conceded that the personage that is called the devil was created an angel of high rank, but by some means has fallen, and became the leader of all wickedness. But was there any sin in the universe before the first angels, one or more became apostates, or could such thing be possible? Could infinite goodness originate sin? No, impossible; such thing could not come to pass.

Then, if creative authority could not originate sin without sacrificing truth and justice, and love and mercy, undeifying self-existent deity and destroying his power to create—for nothing less than infinite purity and perfection can possess the power to create—if, then, the great Almighty did create men and angels, who afterward sinned and fell, could it be possible that the entire future of those angels and men that fell was not known to the Creator as perfect before they were created, as it can be known after the whole of these vast events have come to pass? Such possibility would destroy the perfections of Godhead.

But seeing all the consequences of all creatures were known, and the creator endowed the element, that has became fallen, with faculties capable of falling and sinning, then the origin of sin and of their fall must be found to be elsewhere than in the creature. For if the creature originated sin, then, as a matter of immovable truth, the entire consequence of the origin of wrong and sin falls back primarily on the Creator, who endowed them with ability to produce such results. Here, then, in the light of Bible teaching, and in the light of reason and truth, there is but one conclusion possible, and that conclusion is that the fall of angels and men, or the human race, was produced by the origin of sin as set forth in the fourth chapter of this writing.

Wrong interpretations will make darkness in anything that is written. Why should it be contended for, that wrong must have had an active, intelligent agent to produce it, or to be the originating cause of it? Why not rather admit the idea that wrong as well as right, is eternal? The right was inherent in self-existent Deity, and it was, and is productive of all righteousness, but could not produce wickedness or sin, or evil. But the wrong that was eternal had not any active, intelligent agent that could develop it until created intelligence would exist, but was like fire, the nature or principle of which exists alike everywhere; but to make it useful it must be developed by the aid of suitable material. So the principle of wrong could not be developed without the aid of suitable material, which was created agents, whether spiritual or physical. But the principle of right cannot produce wrong or evil. Neither can the principle of wrong produce righteousness or good. Wrong is the enemy of all nature. Hence, the propriety of preparing to meet, and bring that enemy under divine control before anything could be created that the enemy could contaminate. And the installation of the Commander, that must reign till he hath put all enemies under his feet, was the inauguration of the war. But after that was established by an unchangeable decree, then the Atoner and the Commander could create all things. Treated in chapter

1. Hence, that adverse principle in nature, which was the antagonist of the source of all righteousness and all goodness, was the germ from which all sin and all evil were originated and perpetuated. It is all the fruit of the great principle, wrong. To overcome that enemy, the warfare was a real necessity. It could not be overcome only in the hands of its friends; for carnal weapons must meet spiritual weapons until the power of that universal enemy would be brought to an end everlastingly. But to overcome that enemy, its developments was an absolute necessity, and this is the reason why the great Commander permitted the enemy to produce the fall of angels and men, that the other extermination of the enemy's power might be secured. Then their falls are not mysteries, neither do they lack reason or logic, but are as clear philosophy as that fire produces heat, or burns. But none can fall, save by voluntary choice, and everyone will reap that which he willingly sows.

It has been the speculation of many, since my memory serves me, as to what would have been the condition of men if they had remained perfect, holy, pure. Some think that if angels nor men had fallen that man would have remained in perfect bliss on this planet everlastingly.

Others advance the idea that the whole race would have been sinless, and would not have suffered but live in perfect happiness until the old structure would be worn out, and then pass into endless bliss without suffering. Various other theories have been advanced, but what better is any or all of this than infidelity? For if this world and the human race had not been natural necessities to do the work that they have done, are doing, and will do, then they would not ever have been seen, they would not at all. For if the Creator is perfect and immutable in power and in knowledge and wisdom, and as perfect in love and mercy, truth and justice, then it is impossible that this or any other planet could exist any other way than to accomplish the purpose for which it was designed in creation. Then the question might arrise, "Does not this make the Creator the author of sin?" But that has been already answered. The Creator cannot produce, nor cause to be produced, anything wrong or sinful. But his enemy does produce all the evil and sin in nature, and the Creator suffers so much and no more as will serve for its own entire overthrow. But the infidel asks, "why does not the Lord appear for the rescue of his own struggling people, and also to rescue the millions whose minds the enemy holds in a spiritual prison and leads them captive at his will?"

That inquiry is answered by the events of the war of insurrection in America. There were a number of places in the South that were called prisons. Those prisoners that the South would take from the North would be put in those prisons and so inhumanly treated that many of them chose death, and sought death, and the accounts of cruelty shocked the country from center to circumference. But could the national authorities not have released them? Yes, they had the power to recall the army and acknowledge the Southern government. The next day would have released all the prisoners, but they could not release those sufferers without abandoning the object of the war.

Neither can the great Commander release those whose spirits are held in prison, nor can he release the soldier of the cross until the ends of wisdom and necessity are accomplished. The enemy must be overcome by a fair hand to hand fight. Then every one will receive his reward. The Lord did not suffer men to grow wicked that he might make a display of His power in their destruction. But those who choose the ways of wickedness are suffered to do so just so far as their wickedness can be made to answer an absolutely necessary purpose and no farther.

The great Commander in this vast warfare has the most unconditional control of, and over, everything in nature that was created, and over all the work that any, or all creatures can or do perform, be they good or bad. But an uncreated principle that is not intelligent, not active, and can only act in one direction, such principle being eternal in its nature, is not subject to the control of any power, but the evil it produces is like the creature, it is subject to the Divine control.

It is clear that if the great eternal King would have a perfect kingdom and a perfect government, he must subdue that natural enemy, and as the enemy was a vast one, it requires a vast warfare for its overthrow, and that warfare was inaugurated as far back in the period of the past as we find the name of Jesus Christ installed as ruler and commander, and that is from everlasting, Micah. 1 and 2, and also eternal, Ephesians 3:11. It is taught clear as anything can be, both in the old and new testament, that the great Commander does possess the most absolute power and authority over all created nature. But the human race must carry the warfare through on the principles of free agency, and all choose the side of the army to join. Then the wicked element is as essential to bring the wrong where the soldier of the cross can overcome it, as the soldier of the cross is needful to overcome it. But everything that could be done to save the agents and not destroy their agency, the Lord has done. Hence he says, "what could have been done more to my vineyard that I have not done it?" Isaiah 5:4 and Daniel 12:2, "And many of them that sleep in the dust of the earth shall awake, some to everlasting life, and some to shame and everlasting contempt." Third verse: "And they that be wise shall shine as the brightness of the firmament; and they that turn many to righteousness as the stars for ever and ever."

What vast inducements are offered to those that turn a sinner from the error of his way, who "shall save a soul from death, and shall hide a multitude of sins," besides the rewards offered to those that bring the wanderer back. We have the Lord's desire toward the wicked that they would turn; as in Ezekiel 33:11, "He delights not in the death of the wicked, but rather they would turn and live." Lamentations 14:33, "For He doth not afflict willingly, nor grieve the children of men." 1st Timothy, second and third verse, "Who will have all men to be saved, and to come unto the knowledge of the truth." And 2d Peter, 14:9, "Not willing that any perish, but that all should come to repentence." Hence it is the Lord cannot righteously save the sinner only by his own agency, and it grieves Him at His heart to see agents make bad choice. But "There is joy in heaven over one sinner that repenteth." For righteousness will result in life and happiness, just as wickedness will result in endless misery, despair and hopeless death. And these results follow these causes as naturally as cause produces effect in any thing in nature.

CHAPTER VI.

THE WARFARE.

When the War was Inaugurated, and its Nature:

Chapter one shows natural necessity for the great war of the universe, in which this planet and the human race are engaged, and the sole purpose and design of the existence of the human race, or for a sinful race. The teaching of the Bible, directly and indirectly, shows this warfare with such force that its meaning cannot be mistaken, and all nature conspires to bear testimony to the same fact.

As far back as we can find, the name and personage of Jesus Christ, that far back we must consider him in conection with this world and the human race, reigning in all the realm of this planet, and over its inhabitants, after he had created them. And he must reign until he hath put all enemies under his feet. 1st Cor., chapter 15 and verse 25. The commencement of his reign and of the warfare may be found at, or near the same period. There are many expressions in the old testament that put that event the same as the new testament, that is before all things. Micah, 5th chapter and 2d verse, says: "He was from everlasting," and Eph. 3 and 11, says: "According to the eternal purpose which he purposed in Christ Jesus, our Lord." So far back was all his work appointed to him by an unchangeable decree and could not be omitted or be a failure, and this Ruler and Commander in the warfare, being installed in these offices, was the inauguration of the war.

The Bible puts the ratification of the atonement and all its connected work of the warefare under his rule and command; all, before there was any created thing in existence, either planet or agent. But after he was ordained commander and atoner, he was creator of all things. This leaves us with no need of any further testimony that the enemy to be subdued was a natural one, self-existent as Deity, and was not subject to the divine command like all created nature. Hence, the necessity of a war to overcome the power and the work of the natural enemy.

To make any war a success, the fighting element, or the soldiers, are an indispensible necessity, and human beings are the soldiers for that spiritual warfare. But another necessity is a commander, and our Jesus is the great Commander-in-chief, and meets all necessities. But in this warfare another equal necessity was an atonement for sin, for the entire race, that would fall in the person of the first pair, for that warfare could not be carried on by pure hands, on pure ground. The evil must meet the good or it could not be overcome, and the Commander undertakes the atonement.

From the initiation of the race, by whom the warfare would be fought and finished, the enemy's work was displayed in producing the fall of the first pair. Everything from the commencement shows that the commander and Lord of the righteous army designed making a perfect work of the warfare, for he permitted the enemy to bring the entire race under his banners in the person of the first pair. He was the strong man armed, and would fain have kept the palace and his goods in peace. But the great Commander is the stronger, that came upon him, and overcame him and has divided the spoils. But the fight was not to commence yet. The Commander takes his soldiers from the ranks of the enemy and thus divides the spoils, and disciplines them the next four thousand years. After that the Commander-in-chief comes to the field in person, and so soon as he acquired the lawful age he entered the battle ground and commenced active service in the hand to hand fight, first by fulfilling all obligations when he was initiated into the priesthood.

He armed himself with perfect obedience by fulfilling the law of consecration, for the priest was washed with water at the door of of the tabernacle, not in water; Ex. xxix:4. Jesus was washed at the door of the Christian dispensation by his baptism in Jordan. And the priest was anointed with the emblem of the Holy Ghost; Ex. xxix:7. But

Jesus, after his washing, received the anointing by the Holy Ghost in reality. The dove lit on him. Then, being armed for the conflict, the next account is that he was in the wilderness and met the champion of wrong hand to hand, but conquered him.

All the time he was with his followers, he instructed them by example and by precept to meet evil with good, and hatred with love, and to meet wrong with right in all cases, using spiritual weapons against carnal weapons. When he was arrested one of his disciples took the sword, but the Lord forbade it, and healed the wound that was made on his enemy; and gave his disciples to know that more than twelve legions of angels were at his command; but they must overcome with spiritual weapons, good for evil. The enemy thought to overcome him when they put him to death, but the greatest conquest that ever was gained in the universe, was gained at the moment of our Savior's death. And with these arms, or spiritual weapons, the followers of the great Commander are gaining victories, and will until the spirit of Christ has overcome all opposition.

When we consider in the light of the Bible the nature of the warfare, and also, in the light of the experience of the church, and of the world up to the present time, it is essentially right against wrong. The soldiers of the cross are led by him whose they are; and him that redeemed, and bought them with his own blood. Their weapons are entirely spiritual, not carnal, and to be clothed or armed with the spirit of their leader, is the only armor that can or that ever did gain a permanent conquest. But the appearance sometimes is as though the whole world, including the church, was using carnal weapons, as when Eligah, the prophet, thought that all were gone over to Baal, and himself alone was left, and they sought his life, but there were a few left then. But again, in the days of the French revolution, so universal became the carnal weapon that they thought they had destroyed the last Bible, and a Christian must not be suffered within the limits of the government. But when in either case they would find man or woman, young or old, with no visible means of defense, they would with their carnal weapons put them to death. The signal victory was to those who, like their Lord, gave their life willingly for the truth's sake, and were faithful unto death. When they are dead, their blood speaketh. But the spirit of malice cannot conquer malice, either with or without arms, and never did. But when the spirit of Christ is seen in man or woman, malice trembles before it, and often will run from it, and often hide from it; but if the same person would meet malice, with malice, he could have no power at all. But some seem to think that there are none in the world who possess this spirit of Christ, or so few, if any.

What can they do? Yes, they are the small minority. But there are a few, and always has been, who were true with all their ability. These, under their Lord, have conquered the world, and are now coquering the world, and ultimately will conquer the world through Christ. But an exceedingly more dangerous circumstance, wherein is danger of a universal apostasy, is that where the government secures to all liberty of conscience, and when and where religion is popular, people think it honorable to belong to church, and whatsoever grows into public favor can be christened and brought into the church. The church and the world can go to church together, and go to any place of amusement together, and conscience is treated with disdain, and the cross not mentioned or known. And the person that the people can find no fault in, must be crucified as in (John xix:6) their good name, or in their business, or in their property, or reputation, or any way, but put them down. These things make the Christian path narrower than it can be made by the monarchical power, or persecution, or poverty, or sickness, or loss of property, or for friends to turn enemies without cause. Let any one live under such circumstances, and let him give his attention to securing a good conscience, and he will likely be surprised to know that there is perhaps not one within his knowledge to sympathize with him. But his weapons are not carnal, but mighty through God to the pulling down of strongholds.

The most perfect record of the Christian's armor is found in the fifth, sixth and seventh chapters of Matthew, called the sermon on the mount. And though that sets forth a very high rule of action, and of perfection, and some think, flesh and blood never can attain it, yet the Bible makes no lower rule of action than is made in the sermon on the mount.

When the soldiers have the perfect armor and will stand firm with it, it is then that they are perfectly unconquerable. Victory is certain, for their commander is in the field; though he was dead, behold he is alive forever more. And when one or more of his soldiers put on the whole armor and stand firm and loyal until death, behold the Commander is with them, and it is easier for heaven and earth to part than those soldiers to fail of victory.

But does any one dispute that there was and is a warfare on this planet? And if there manifestly is a vast war extending from the fall of man to the present time, and growing warmer and more fierce, then, if infinite power and wisdom created this planet, did He not design it for the very work it is doing? Or has the world deceived the Lord, and gathered the vast majority of the race into the ranks of wickedness, and is holding them there in defiance of creative power? Surely the Lord was not deceived in the work the world is doing. But a few passages to support the truth that Christ and his servants are engaged in a warfare: Luke x:18, "I behold Satan as lightning fall from heaven." Luke xi:21, 22, "When a strong man armed keeps his palace, his goods are in peace; but when a stronger than he shall come upon him and overcome him, he taketh from him all his armor wherein he trusted and divideth his spoils." John xii:31, "Now is the judgment of this world; now shall the prince of this world be cast out." John xvi:11, " Of judgment because the prince of this world is judged." John xiv:30, "For the prince of this world cometh and hath nothing in me."—Agreeing with Genesis iii:15, "It shall bruise thy head and thou shalt bruise his heel." 68th Psalm, verse 18: "Thou hast ascended on high, thou hast led captivity captive." Also, Eph., iv:8; Col., ii:15, "And having spoiled principalities and powers he made a show of them openly, triumphing over them in it." Heb., xi:14, "That through death he might destroy him that had the power of death, that is the devil." Rev. ix:1, "And the fifth angel sounded, and I saw a star fall from heaven into the earth; and to him was given the key of the bottomless pit." And much more. Rev., xii:7, 8, "And there was war in heaven; Michael and his angels fought against the dragons, and the dragons fought and his angels, and prevailed not; neither was their place found any more in heaven. And the great dragon was cast out, that old serpent called the devil and satan, which deceiveth the whole world, and he was cast out into the earth, and his angels were cast out with him."

Now, if Bible is testimony, then, surely, we are in the midst of a war, and if the perscutions of the pure worshippers are brought to view, how many millions of Christian men and women, young and old, lay down their lives willingly on the altar of truth and righteousness for their Lord's sake? The warfare was fierce and terrible then, but every life so laid down was a conqueror.

Our risen Lord in sending his messages to the seven churches, closed each of the seven, with a promise "to him that overcometh."

But there is a day and also a year mentioned when the great leader will take hold of this warfare in a more terrible manner. Isaiah, xxxvi:8, "For it is the day of the Lord's vengeance and the year of recompenses for the controversy of Zion."

In closing this chapter on warfare, it is observable: that the why and wherefore of this planet or for its existance as it is, has not found a clear solution, and it has seemed one of the darkest questions in theology. Because any observer can see that all nature is so filled with design, and there is no design among men but that can be traced to a designer, and the designs seen in nature are so much brighter than does or can characterize the works of man, therefore wisdon asks, "Is there a possibility for nature to exist without a designer?" and the answer is, "No, it cannot." But another difficulty meets us about the existence of this earth as we see it, and that is how could the Lord create this world with the perfect knowledge of what its inhabitants would do in reference to their fall, and all their sin, and the everlasting punishment? If he knew all before creation, and that must make him the author of sin and of all suffering both in this world, and in the world of endless despair if there was not real necessity for it in some way.

If the Lord does really hate sin, and all things in nature were subject to his word, as really as his word could bring forth a planet, then how could sin exist under his dominion? But if the Lord created this planet very good, and an enemy has come and originated sin, and captured the first pair, and in them the entire human race, and has held so vast a majority of the world in wickedness in every age of the world, then where is the security that that wicked will not finally triumph and rule the world everlastingly? And it is plain that the utter lack of a logical answer to that and several other leading questions, has produced uneasy restlessness, all over the religious world and has induced many great minds to take issue with the Bible, and to hew out for themselves other cisterns that could hold no water, other systems in which there was no rest for their anxious spirit.

But in the light of these several chapters are not all these difficulties made plain and easy? And are not these introductory chapters in clear harmony with the Bible? If they cannot be condemned by the Bible, but do agree with the whole of the scripture, and will bring light and reason in all passages that have been considered dark and mysterious, then why not receive the thoughts and help to make a better improvement of them, until the slander shall be lifted off the Bible and its author, and the infidel left without an inch of room to wheel on? For surely it has been shown that these things were necessary for the success of the war; and were all perfectly provided for in creation. But creative power never produced sin, yet when the very power that the war was brought against; (no matter who was the agent); came to tempt the first pair to sin, notice the armor they were funrished with. It was, "God hath said, we shalt not." This weapon in the hand of that woman could faithfully resist and conquer all the powers for wrong in nature. It was unconquerable. But temptation prevailed and they fell. That is a sample of all sin. It is the work of the enemy but not of the Lord.

CHAPTER VII.

OLD TESTAMENT TYPES.

The types of the Old Testament have been so little considered, and so little effort made to understand them, that they appear to very many, like a mass of ridiculous trash, for which no sense or meaning can be found. The orthodox minister has failed to show them up in the light of reason and actual necessity. They have furnished the strongest hold for the infidel of al most any other, and the Christian world seems to let them go on quietly as though they could not defend the Bible at that point. That I think a sinful error.

For if the types are considered with the vigilence that their merit demands, they will be found to be the clearest exhibition of wisdom on record, and the book of revelation could not be perfect without them. But why so? Because these types are the official records of the legislative authority of a government. But that government was executed with such ability and wisdom that they are the most perfect type of a christian life, the legal acts were passed mostly all. about fourteen hundred years before the Christian era. But those types show with perfect clearness the duty of man to his Lord, and also to all men. But the more excellent feature of these types is that they show so unerringly the highness of men's calling, and the exaltedness of their privilege in Christ. But most valuable of all they show the fullness and excellency of the atonement in all its minutive, and the type of the kingdom of Christ set up in the heart, in which none but Christ should reign, and show how pure the heart must be in which to erect the throne where the King will bear rule. That is shown by the type that looks darkest and is most objected to, and least defended, but nevertheless is one of the richest passages of the Bible, and that is the extermination of the inhabitants of the land of promise, whether east or west of Jordan, and also the Midianites. But look at this with rational eyes, and common sense view, and it is one of the most excellent writings on earth. The extermination of the Midianites was a type. Here let me speak to the infidel that thinks this narrative so perfectly insupportable in the light of logical reason. Israel was a type of something from the call of Abraham to the present time. The people came passively into bondage in Egypt; that is, people are born into the world in sin, without their agency. But when the Israelites were brought from that bondage, that is a type of a soul being converted from sin to grace, from darkness to light. When the Israelites were at Paran, they were told to go over and possess the land. But they thought the inhabitants too strong for them, they would not go. This is the

Christian. In due time after conversion, they see in the word of promise their privilege to inherit a pure and perfect heart, the Lord will help to drive his and their enemies out of their heart, that he may dwell there. But the fearful one says in his heart, "My enemies are too strong for me, my pride, my malice, my love of the world, or its fashions, or its habits; and many other things so opposite to the spirit of Christ, I cannot go to possess the land at this time." But when the Lord turned Israel into another course to go through the wilderness forty years, and not to see the promised land until they would cross the Jordan, that is the Christian who refuses to leave the world and cleanse the Lord's temple of his heart, that Christ should dwell in it, and that he might live in the spirit of heaven, while on earth. But such have yet afforded them one possible chance, one possible hope: That was to fight and conquer until the Jordan is crossed, or if not that, then fall in the wilderness and never see the salvation of the Lord. When Israel had struggled and fought through until they came near the Midianites, so near through their journey, it is likely the most interesting period of their history. To help them along to their journey's end safely, would secure to them the promised land; but to lead them into idolatry, licentiousness and corruption, was their utter and hopeless ruin and despair.

The sin into which Israel was led by the Midianites resulted in the fall of 24,000 of them of Israel, but Midian was not yet touched.

Israel led into sin by Midian, is the Christian, who having fought well nigh through the wilderness, meets some influential parties that lead him into sin. This type is like meridian sun light to all the world that will turn a Christian out of the way of Godliness, into sin and ruin. Without a miracle there is but one fate for such, and that is hopeless despair. Is it not the clearest logic that the example should have been made of Midian that was made? Physically they were utterly destroyed except the women children. The objection the infidel makes to this is absolutely without common sense. The Midianites, who were enemies in the war, had rendered themselves so corrupt that justice required their destruction; but they were held until a wise use could be made of them. They sustained the relation to the Lord and his government that the traitor and deserter does to a political government when it is warring with another nation. Where, then, is the disputer that boldly asserts this to be the darkest chapter in nature? But, O man, to whom do you speak these false words? Is not this among the very lightest chapters in nature, whether in or out of the Bible? Nor was it ever repeated, but one act of the kind was a real necessity to teach so important a lesson, and to make revelation. But you may say, "Could not all these things have been taught by precept, and not require this wholesale slaughter of human beings?" Yes, oh, yes; and it has been taught by words plain and easy. But it is like when the snake, or the devil, whichever did tempt the woman to eat the forbidden fruit; the woman said, "God hath said we shall not." But the serpent covered over what God had said with his own words, and gave it the lie, and induced her to commit the sin. In like manner, the infidel, cunning as the snake, will cover the words that God hath said with his own words, and with a lie, and make the world believe that the words of scripture mean anything but what they do mean.

If this type is consulted the pilgrim can see that what God hath said is true, and the infidel can see as plainly his doom, and none can go to the judgment blinded. That one case of the Midianites, and a similar order in case of the Canaanites and the Amalekites are all the exterminating orders the Lord ever issued against physical nature, and the last is logical as the first. The Lord commanded that when the Israelites should drive the heathen out of the promised land, they should leave alive nothing that breatheth. No such order has ever been issued before or since. But why would the God of the Bible issue such command respecting the Canaanites? Surely it is easily seen. The land was given by an everlasting covenant for an everlasting possession, as a type, until Christ should come, and then give way to the anti-type that should be everlasting, reaching into the eternal world, where nothing less than perfect purity can abide. The natural land must be a perfect type of the spiritual land. It might be observed here that the inhabitants of Canaan were so corrupt that utter destruction was the only fit condition for them. But Wisdom held them until the wisest use could be made of them. Their treason made them a lawful prey when they would be useful. Now these corrupt heathens that inhabited the land of promise were the fittest type of the indwelling principles of the unchanged heart. As the order was to destroy those heathens, leaving alive nothing that breatheth, it is a perfect type of preparing the human heart for the spiritual kingdom, for the reign of the infinitely pure and holy Lord Christ, that is, turn everything else out, but the King that is to reign therein. But some of the tribes failed to drive out or exterminate the heathen entirely, and hence, were very soon led by them into trouble and sin and bondage. When they would repent and call on the Lord he sent them deliverance; but their affinity with the heathen led them into sin so repeatedly that the Lord sent Israel into hopeless exile, and they became mingled among the heathen, and their nationality lost. This is the fittest type of Christians who assume to go into the promised land, which is, under Christ, the sanctified heart and life; but when they fail to turn the world perfectly out of their hearts and lives, the worldly principle that is suffered to remain, prohibits the reign of Christ and leads them into the world and wickedness, and except a miracle is wrought, they will, like Israel be hopelessly lost.

But when one steps into the fullness of the liberty of Christ's children in the gospel and is a co-worker with Christ to drive all the buyers (John ii, 14–16) and sellers out of the temple of his heart, and erect the Redeemer's throne there, and himself stand sentinel day and night to guard and keep that heart, such an one lives in heaven while on earth; and when the war is over with him, like the man Moses, he is found on the mountain height, and the promised land in sight, and he enters on to his promised inheritance, but does not come in sight of Jordan.

But the infidel that has said these narratives are without reason or explanation, that they are cruel, merciless, and not worthy of such character as the God of the Bible is represented to be, might he not well be ashamed? And you, minister of the cross, that have conceded these narratives to be real difficulties, how have you helped the enemies of the cross, when the argument is at hand to defend the cross and the Bible and its author?

These wars of extermination have seemed the darkest passages of the Bible, but here is logical reason that settles a few thoughts, and revelation could not be perfect without these very narratives. The exhibition of truth and justice, love and mercy that is shown in these narratives cannot be excelled in the light of clear, logical reason. In all political wars the crime of treason, joining the opposite army, is death, and it seems right in the eyes of every person. The well deserved penalty only was exercised on these nations. The same is due to treason to all nations or men. Another indispensible cause for the types of the Old Testament was and is for the discipline of the Christian army, the soldier of the cross.

When men go into the army of their country as soldiers they must be taken through a disciplinary course before they are fit for the field. What is the propriety of that? It is that they may be skilled in handling and using arms, bayonet against bayonet, and sword against sword, and all secular weapons against the same character of arms; to obey, command, and to endure the life and hardships of a soldier. Nor are the services of a soldier in any department of the army nearly as valuable if they have not been well disciplined. If it then requires a costly disciplining to prepare men to meet arms with the same kind of arms, where all visible prospects are as favorable for them as for their opponents, how much more, and more thorough, is the disciplining needful for a small army to subdue the world without any visible weapons of warfare? But love must contend against hatred, and good against evil, and right against wrong. The soldiers must be skilled in the use of these weapons, so that their victory is sure. Pray for them that do you a private injury, or that destroy your good name, or your property. Return good and kind treatment to those that maliciously treat you. The discipline for perfect obedience is found in Abraham's obedience in leaving his kindred and country and going into a strange land; and again, when he was commanded to sacrifice his son, and so promptly obeyed. But the soldiers need discipline to endure hardness. That is seen in Joseph being kept in prison unjustly so long, and how the Lord overruled it; and again, when Israel was in bondage so oppressive, but suffered the will of the Commander. But Christians are disciplined, or at what cost of disobedience is shown, by the Israelites not going over to possess the land when they were commanded to do so; they died in the wilderness. It is shown again when the Midianites led them into disobedience, and the plague slew twenty-four thousand of them. But the discipline to trust for deliverance from danger, as at crossing the Red Sea and the river Jordan; the discipline to trust for sustenance, as when they were fed by manna, and drank of the stream that flowed from the rock; the discipline to be perfect, pure, holy, and correspondingly strong; all that is seen in the utter extermination of the Canaanites, who represent the natural inhabitants of the human heart. These, like the Canaanites, must be utterly exterminated or no success. But it would be tedious to mention all the items that the Christian soldier finds in the Old Testament types; but in those types the discipline is perfect for the Christian; and if there were no other use for the Old Testament, the Bible could not be perfect without this. But the unparalleled grandeur of it is, that any one item it was designed to show, was done as fully, as richly and grandly, as if there had been no other object to be reached but itself. But there were many other objects of equal importance to be accomplished by the same scripture at the same time, and every one of them is accomplished as perfectly as it could have been, had it been the only one, noticed more in other chapters. The hand to hand fight did not commence during the four thousand years before Christ, but the forces were being drilled and prepared for action when the Commander should come to the field.

Some persons tell us the Bible is not true; and a prominent part of their argument is, that the Commander of the right against wrong, gave commands in a few cases to make necessary example of treason, by commanding the utter destruction of the heathen from the land of promise; and also of the Midianites and the Amalekites and the people of Sodom. These cases were not simply to show the punishment of treason, but the really necessary exercise of discipline. This is so plain that none can be blind to these truths but those who will not see. These same persons will readily acknowledge that the commander of an army could not make a success if he did not exercise discipline closely; that without rigorous ruling any army would become ungovernable, disloyal, divided; and their better disciplined enemies would make an easy prey of them and their cause. If the Major Andres would come into the army of the revolution and conspire with the Arnolds to defeat and destroy the army, and the cause for which they fought, and the General Washington in the case would give no attention to the treason and conspiracy, nor bring to justice the guilty parties within their reach; in such a case, these same objectors to the Bible would say such an officer ought to be put to death, and his example should be one of the most severe character. But here was a few cases of discipline, just enough to meet necessities and no more, but of millions fold more weight and importance than treason in a political army can be, and yet men of rational brain will condemn the Bible because of them. Oh, is consistency a jewel, and is common sense worth exercising?

CHAPTER VIII.

GOSPEL FAITH.

The faith of the Gospel should not be considered dark or mysterious. Surely nothing in nature is more reasonable or logical, for the principle is seen in all pursuits of the world. If any person fully believes that Christ is more to him than all things else in nature, that person will be loyal to Christ with all the physical and mental power he possesses. The faith that does not make its possessor faithful is a deception. Faith itself is without value or power or merit, but perfect loyalty to the Lord will produce the best and most faithful service that its possessor can render; that which unites the servant to his Lord in the relation of father and son, or daughter, and the children are heirs to the father's possession. Hence, if faith saves its possessor, it does it on the logical principles of cause and effect. Loyalty or fidelity cannot be produced without faith in the object to which the party is loyal; neither can the loyalty be perfect when there is more than one object of faith. As the Lord has told us, we cannot serve God and mammon. Many come to a point in their history where Christ on the one hand, and the world on the other, invite their attention. Christ has many claims, and much to admire, but the world is here, visible, with all its charms and its necessities. To choose one is to reject the other, and the faith that governs the life must make the decision. Some see Christ in such excellency that their faith and heart and life decide entirely in his favor. Such sacrifice the world with all its prospects, its facinations, its pleasures. Their faith takes hold of Christ in perfect fidelity and loyalty. This constitutes them God's people, and entitles them to his promise to be their God; Ezekiel, xxxvi:28; and each party is owned by the other party alike, with all they have, and with all they are. Now the adopted child recognizes his Lord's presence constantly. He fasts and prays and does his alms in secret, and his Father rewards him openly. It is cause and effect in every particular. If the Lord honors such individuals with some work that looks miraculous, it is in the clearest sense cause and effect. The Spirit makes the impression on the mind what to do or what to ask for, and the Lord does the work. The cause and the effect are plain alike, as when the five-year old child says, "Papa, lift me over the fence." The father reaches over the top of the fence and lifts the child over. Now, if the act of the child was seen, but the power not visible, the miracle would be as notable as those that the Lord performs by his faithful children. In all this there is no mystery. But faith is a mystery when one chooses the world but professes faith in Christ, yet never possesses it, or never shows its fruits. Such persons boast of it oftener and more than those who do possess it; and often kindle a fire and compass themselves about with sparks. Isaiah 1:11 But our Lord has told us the fate of these. They will go deceived to the very judgment and tell the Lord they had prophesied in his name, and cast out devils, and done many wonderful works. But they will hear that awful word, "Depart, I never knew you," or ye that work iniquity. When faith is professed by them that choose the world it is a mystery, but the Christian should not suffer it to be called a mystery.

In the very nature of things it is and ever was impossible to save the fallen and sinful by any other means; justice would forbid it, for it is impossible to save the disloyal and be just; and there is nothing that can produce loyalty to Christ, or anything else, without faith in the object to which the subject should be loyal. Hence the faith that possesses and controls the entire heart and life for its Lord that unites its possessor to the spiritual body of which Christ is the head; and to be thus united, that is the salvation.

Then God can be just and the justifier of him which believeth in Jesus, and justice could not save on any other principle or condition. The whole subject may be fitly illustrated by considering all the pursuits of the whole earth. Whatever the plan that any intelligent mind puts into practice, it is faith that decides the kind of work to be done.

There is no person engages in any thing until he believes that thing to be best for him, everything considered. Though some may not be pursuing the calling of their choice, yet in such a case, it is because there is something which prevents their doing so. Now that which they do is their faith, and it is known by their actions that it produces. But if circumstances should change, so that some other calling would be more satisfactory to them, everything considered, and their best judgment so decides, they are as sure to change as cause produces effect, and it is because their faith prefers the new to the old. The same principle holds good in the marriage relation. When two individuals join their destiny in marriage, both in good faith, they will be contented, and remain so till death, if they remain in good faith toward each other. But if they grow weary of each other, and find some other that they prefer before their lawful companion, their affections will be divided, and they will desire all obstacles to be removed that hinders them from changing companions; and when both parties are fully convinced that, everything considered, a change would be best, and their faith fully endorses the idea, they are as sure to make the change if they can, as the rain is sure to fall when it is discharged from the cloud. Just as logically and as certainly, when people's faith takes hold of the Lord Christ, their service will be loyal and perfect, and remain so until their faith in him fails.

Now what has more common sense reason, or clearer logic than the Christian faith, Gospel faith, the faith that saves and the faith without which there can be no salvation? Let the whole earth blush to call it a mystery, or dark. The preacher who fills a high official place in church with a high salary, who studies only enough to perform the work assigned to him, and spends his time among the proud and worldly, that man cannot explain the Christian faith to his congregation. To him it is a mystery. But ask the perfectly devoted person, old or young, the meat and drink of whose spirit is to live and walk in the Lord, ask such an one to explain the nature of saving faith, and though he may not be ready to give a logical answer, he will be likely to give an answer that will embrace the sentiment herein described.

CHAPTER IX.

REWARDS AND PUNISHMENTS.

They are the result of cause and effect.
Nature of fire, spiritual.
It is seen in this life.
Fire and brimstone are figurative.
The everlasting punishment, Math. xxv : 46. Is the doctrine mystery, or is it not the inevitable result of cause and effect? For guilt as the fuel, feeds memory as the fire; and a sense of hopeless loss, with conscience as the gnawing worm that dieth not, shows that it was the willful choice of the subjects to fight against their Lord and his righteousness, and hazzard the consequences. The Lord's messengers that were sent to plead with them to accept life, whether the messenger was the word preached, or whether it was conscience, or the pleadings of friends, or the example of the righteous life, all were alike treated with contempt. The Almighty was mocked, and the ways of death were chosen in spite of God and man. Added to this must be of necessity, the awful realization that this state is changeless and eternal. These faculties, memory and conscience, are not physical, but they are faculties of the spirit, and cannot die nor cease to exist, and the Bible, as well as reason, teaches that material fire cannot affect the spirit; neither

does the fire that preys on the spirit affect the material body, only as the spirit is more powerful than the material body. When the spirit is crushed or broken, the body often fails under it; but when the body fails, if the spirit is in favor with the Lord, producing a good conscience, it will grow stronger while life endures. As fire and brimstone so signally affect the natural body the chief design of their existence in nature is to convey the idea that the spiritual fire will in like manner affect the spirit. For these logical reasons, the everlasting punishment in the nature of things necessarily must be the effect of causes that the sufferers themselves have worked out, and for which there is no being in the universe responsible but those alone that suffer the penalty.

Rev. vii : 9, 14 tell us of a great multitude that have washed their robes and made them white in the blood of the Lamb. These are the saved of the earth, and the reason why others are not saved is because their filthy robes were not washed. As the filth of those robes is of spiritual character, and the robe is the outer garment, it seems clear that the wicked actions, and words, and influences, all wickedness of every kind that has filled up the life, will be seen in the robe, visible to the inhabitants of all worlds, which is the very nature of sin and wrong, showing that there is no power over, nor remedy for sin in the universe only the divine power, and no provision only that which Christ has made. Every sin of thought, word or deed of the whole life of those that reject the offer of mercy will be a spot in their robe, and every spot will show the crime that produced it. Hence all the sin of the world must be exposed to all the universe everlastingly. That will make good the fourth chapter of Mark, verse 22, and other passages. For there is nothing hid that shall not be manifested, neither was anything kept secret, but that it should come abroad. Here is the logical fulfillment of Daniel xii : 2; Many of them that sleep in the dust of the earth shall awake, some to everlasting life, and some to shame and everlasting contempt.

Now, inasmuch as the Lord has given certain special qualities to fire and has referred to fire to give an idea of the future state of the lost, there is then, the strongest support for the doctrine of the everlasting punishment in its most literal sense, and on the logical principles of cause and effect. As to the power that is given to the spiritual fire we cannot be certain. But the shame and everlasting contempt of the sin-stained robes, and the gnawing worm of conscience that dieth not, and the unquenchable fire of memory, with the realization that it is everlasting, must be sufficient to keep the fire of perdition kindled eternally.

There is the strongest evidence under our notice that these spiritual fires burn in the hearts and consciences of many people while they are in sound health physically to such an extent that they seek release from them by suicide, or self-murder. But with some the weight is so vast that it overcomes the powers of life, and they die. About the year 1847 an event occurred that startled the country and was published through eastern Ohio in a long and minute account, to the effect that a man inherited a large and desirable property by his marriage. His wife died, leaving an only child, a little son. The man died, leaving the charge of the son and the property with his brother, who was to put the child in possession of the property when he should come to legal agency; but if the child should die the brother would be heir to the property. That man found convenience to put the boy in the river with a stone hanged about his neck. But the act was seen, and eleven years after the deed was done, the witness and the criminal met, neither knowing of the other. The witness related the narrative to the criminal, and at the end of the narrative the criminal fainted. When he revived he made a full and minute confession of the crime. Three days after that he died, and by his death he escaped a criminal's execution. He could not endure the fire of the spirit.

Another case was published in Davis county, Indiana. A man committed murder, escaped from justice and could not be heard of. But nine years after the deed was done he returned, gave himself up, and confessed the crime. Verily it is a fire that burns. I stayed half a year in Oakland with a friend. A daily published in Oakland came into the house at 7 P. M., giving most of the important news of the civilized world up to noon the same day. A morning sheet from San Francisco was brought at 7 A. M., giving most of the important events of the civilized nations up to midnight before. The striking feature of these daily papers was the great number of suicides that was published in them, and all of them traceable to the fire of the spirit as the cause of their self murder. Verily, it is cause and effect. That the nature of the fire is spiritual, and not physical, is clearly seen from the fact that the five physical senses die with the physical man and cannot live again. But the spirit, the essential part of man, is vastly more sensitive, as well as more powerful, than the physical nature, and the faculties of the spirit must of necessity possess a nature to convey all manner of intelligence to the spirit. The causes that produce misery or comfort to the physical nature cannot affect the disembodied spirit, such as cold or heat, or the sorrows or passions of earth. But like as the fire and brimstone produce quick, sharp sensations to the physical man, so will be the memory and the conscience to the sensitive spirit, memory an unquenchable fire, and conscience the worm that will gnaw without ceasing, yet never die. But these results of the spiritual fire on the spirit, are they not fixed laws in nature and not subject to any power of annihilation? The essential use of fire and brimstone was to instruct man as to what did await the lost soul. The elements of punishment are inherent in the sin, and sinners who would not accept of their opportunity to be cleansed, but retain the sin, retain with it the elements of their punishment. So that the doctrine of the everlasting punishment rests on the fixed laws of cause and effect as plainly as that cause will produce effect in any department of nature.

There is not a rational minded being in nature that could say other than that the elements of wickedness should be separated from all the elements of purity, and when they are thus set off from all purity and confined to safe limits, themselves and their own nature from the elements of hell, and do literally justify all the language used in the scripture describing it. If these elements of wickedness would be suffered to roam through nature at will their ambition would be to contaminate every planet in the universe as they have contaminated this earth.

"But the righteous into life eternal," and joy eternal, and purity and holiness eternal, and peace and happiness eternal, and the glory of their great Lord everlastingly.

But those who stand on the right hand who go into life eternal, these will be the most distinguished part of the Lord's creation. They will be the veterans of the war, and the fellow soldiers and the fellow sufferers of the King of kings and Lord of lords. They will be brothers, sisters, mothers, of the great commander, and fellow heirs with him of all things.

They will be kings and priests, rulers of cities, and an endless monument of the power that brought them through a world full of sin with garments spotless and pure. These glorified ones will be an endless exhibition of the infinite wisdom that saw before creation the enemy that was in nature and ordained such vast measures for its overthrow, and all attributes of the divine character will be glorified alike thereby. These holy ones will show their creation, and their formation and their fall, and how they were redeemed and washed and made pure. They will be an endless record of the infinite power of their Lord that conquered yonder vast and terrible enemy, and has put it within prison bounds, and cut off its power to work destruction any more at all. And thus all worlds that revolve around the divine throne, the central point of the universe, when they see the nature and magnitude of the enemy, and see the commander and the soldiers that conquered their enemy, will they not exclaim, "Glory to God in the highest?" There is endless necessity for both the righteous and the wicked of this world everlastingly. They are not only philosophical, but an absolute necessity.

CHAPTER X.

DESIGN OF REVELATION. REASON FOR AND USE OF THE BOOK OF REVELATIONS.

If the most essential use of this book lies very far beyond the interests of this planet, and is very different from the benefit of the human race simply, nevertheless its benefits and interests to the human race are none the less valuable, but are of as much value to man as if its sole use were for their benefit, and it is as worthy of fidelity, worship, praise, constancy, loyalty and devotion.

We are informed in revelation that the book of nature reveals to man, light sufficient to make him responsible, and to lead him to the salvation of the Lord. Psalm xix. and Zeph. iii : 5, and Romans i : 19, 20, and also Job, and others, who knew the Lord without revelation. There are vast numbers of the human race that never see written revelation, and how few of those who have it who come up to its spirit and its letter! But those who do, to them the value is incalculable. But what a great proportion of those who have the Bible, show a depravity that they could not show without it? That will go with them into everlasting punishment, and be an endless exhibition that they chose the road to death with the Bible at their pleasure, when and as they chose, and thus will be shown the fruit of wrong in a way that could not be done otherwise. How much of this must the judgment reveal? How has the bible been treated in legislative bodies? How is it treated by the reading public, by the heads of families and in places of education? Do not the great mass of people of any age or sect, hold the Bible to their own condemnation? And those who are numbered among Christians, how many of them read the Bible? When it is ridiculed and held up to the scorn and contempt of all present, who among those professing to believe it are ready to step forth and defend it? Most of them would defend their own character, but not the Bible and its author. But if their governor should send them a letter offering them money or property for its defense, would they be so indifferent about it?

How many ministers of the Gospel are ready to meet the champion infidel, and by showing the strength of the Bible, put its enemies to shame? By the principles of this Bible will all these persons be judged and when they are condemned they will say it is just.

But notice the possibility, the probability, the likelihood, of its use in being held on exhibition everlastingly. All the Lord's creatures will likely be capacitated to read it, and know it, and it will be a revelation of the Lord to all his creatures forever. They will see him in all the attributes of his character, all maintained to infinite perfection. The saved of this world will see it and the last of this world will see it. But the countless myriads of worlds that have never fallen will likely read in revelation the character of their Creator. And of the vast warfare in which their great enemy was met and conquered, and that not one of these divine attributes was impaired or stained to the slightest possible extent.

But when countless periods have gone by and the exhibition of this world shall grow dim in all created memory, and the inhabitants of worlds that had not fallen, shall look at the everlasting punishment and seem to wonder if justice could not release the subjects, then it shall be that revelation which is the record of their probation, and of how they insulted the offers of life will settle all inquiries. Beside that, these that are cast away are naturally, wickedly inclined, while any and all other intelligences but them are naturally inclined to righteousness, and that is the great gulf which cannot be passed.

If the lost souls themselves should grow weary and be inclined to complain or excuse themselves, one look at this revelation would end all complaints, and they would be forced to say their sentence was just. But in the nature of things it required a physical world to make such a revelation as was made here. This being what the Lord designed to make—and he has told us that his word should not pass away—it necessarily was made in wisdom and for a use fully worthy of its author. Many thoughts may probably enter into the use of revelation, after the harvest of this world is gathered and sinning will cease forever. Think for a moment of the vast complication of the great warfare, in which wrong in all its forms and magnitudes is overcome, and where wrong is punished with wrong, and wickedness is overcome by wickedness, and such a vast amount of wickedness is punished with temporal judgements. Has the Lord managed this sinful, warring world from first to last, and not used justice out of its legitimate place sometimes, in very extreme cases? Has mercy grown weak or failed toward any, or has the attribute of love never failed to act? Has not power, wisdom or truth been taxed to a disageable extent? Has the attribute of immutability not changed under some possible cirumstances? How could it be possible that this vastly wicked, treacherous world could be managed through from beginning to end, and none of these attributes be impaired, or has the Almighty not the right by sovereign authority to use any or all of these attributes out of their place, under the pressure of extremely difficult circumstances? No! No!! Oh! No! he has not the right any more than a man has. The principles of right are self existent as deity, and there is no being in the universe that has the right to sacrifice the principles of right to the least possible extent.

This book of revelation will show that every one of these attributes has been preserved to infinite perfection and this will be known and read of all the universe, through all the moving of eternity. This, with many other considerations, shows most conclusively that revelation could not be spared at any period of the future. There have been many opinions indulged in when the seeming dark parts of the Bible were looked into. It has been said that the Lord acted on his sovereign power, on his sovereign authority, and that some works which the Lord has done were not, and could not be in harmony with other works that he has done.

That is a slander. The Lord has never done a work in nature that would not have been right for a man to do, if the man had been capable of ruling, and the Lord had sent him to rule. On the self-same philosophical principles it was right for the Lord to do any thing and everything that he ever has done in nature.

The Lord does his work because it is right. But the fact that the Lord has done any work is not the cause of that work being right; but because his work was right, naturally and philosophically, and was necessary for the accomplishment of the ends of wisdom, that was the cause of his doing anything and all things that he did do. When we read that the Lord's words shall not pass away, Matthew xxiv : 35 and First Peter i : 25, and other passages, then let our feeble, limited minds think of the uses and the benefits of the volume of revelation, to be of endless duration revealing the Lord to all inhabitants of all worlds in all his infinite perfection and purity, the immovable foundation on which the entire universe may safely rest and trust. Now if there were no other use for this world and the human race but to make revelation perfect, would it not abundantly justify the Creator for bringing this planet and human race into existence. Come, wise men, that requires logical reason for everything, come up and tell us, is not this philosophically grand, and fully worthy of infinite wisdom and all goodness? But the world does much more than to make revelation.

Besides all this, can we suppose that our highest stretch of imagination can grasp any reasonable proportion of the benefits that the Lord's revelation will be to the Lord's universe during the endless future?

CHAPTER XI.

AUTHENTICITY IS SELF EVIDENT.

If the Bible is philosophical testimony to its own divine authenticity then it is reliable, but if it can not be shown up in that light it is not reliable.

First. The Bible is in perfect harmony with all nature, and the book of nature proves the book of revelation to be true.

Second. The Bible informs us that there was a war inaugurated in nature against an enemy before creation commenced, by ordaining the atonement, and all other necessities for the prosecution and completion of that war, and the experience of this earth and the human race proves that to be true.

Third. The Bible tells us that all things were created by the atoner, and our eyes behold the work of creation as the Bible tells us it was. The demonstration is clear as it can be.

Fourth. The Bible gives the account of the formation of this planet and its inhabitants, and we see it all. The testimony is clear.

Fifth. The Bible gives the account that sin entered into the world and death by sin, and the experience of every sane mind in the world see that to be a demonstrated fact as the Bible gives it. Sin and death are the experiences of our race.

Sixth. The Bible, in its combined passages, gives the idea beyond dispute that the origin of sin was that enemy against whom the war was inaugurated.

These six items—the ground work of all questions that can concern the human race—are all in perfect harmony with each other and with all other parts of the Bible, and with all nature, and are all sensible demonstrations to all men. No testimony can be stronger on any subject.

Seventh. The Bible is the official records of a political government, written by legislative authority, and it is no more to the validity of its truth who the secretaries were that wrote it than the same question would be if the government journals of the United States were taken to another government to establish a legal point in law. But they have as strong claim to the legal acknowledgement of all political powers as the same records of any other government.

Eighth. When the Bible is shown to be true philosopy, then the prophecies should be valid testimony to infidel as well as Christian, and there can be no stronger testimony, if one hundred reliable persons would testify to the same thing in any court, not so strong as prophecy and fulfillment.

Ninth. When philosophy is seen to be perfect in the Bible, then the miracles are the strongest testimony that can be given on earth for anything.

Tenth. When the Bible and the events it gives are shown to be absolute necessities in nature as is shown in these pages, and that neither the earth nor its inhabitants could exist on any other principles than those the Bible gives which are not only logical and reasonable, but absolute necessities to the very existence of planet or agent, then it is proved above any thing in any political point of view.

Eleventh. The designs so visible in creation and all fulfilling the purposes for which the Bible says they were intended are the strongest possible testimonies of its genuineness and also of its authorship. But notice a few other types somewhat different.

Christianity sets up a system of perfect righteousness and all the language used to describe that principle or system is plain and easily understood, but the craftiness of worldly wisdom perverts it entirely in every particular.

If we find that fourteen or fifteen centuries before the introduction of Christianity there was the political government of a nation administered by the author of Christianity, and such ability of wisdom and power was brought into that administration that it makes an unchangeable type of the Christian system which can not be perverted like the teaching by precept, and those types show the Christian system in every particular, that then would establish the divine authenticity of the Bible. Notice some of these types for it would be a weighty work to write all of them.

These types show the posititive condition of the salvation of any man or all men, and in the teaching of them is involved the eternal destinies of this entire world. Now if these things are shown is there any more proof needed for the divine authenticity of the Bible?

Commence with Abram, but afterward called Abraham.

First. He was called to live a different life and he obeyed; so is the Christian and he obeys.

Second. His faith was tried in the sharpest manner, and he obeyed. The Christian's faith is tried in the sharpest manner for him and he obeys.

Third. When he was in a strange nation the monarch took his wife, but he trusted and the Lord rescued them both. When the Christian is imposed upon by the wicked, if he trusts, the Lord helps them out of trouble.

Fourth. The Lord promised him a land in which a kingdom should be set up for the Lord, the plainest type possible of the kingdom set up in the Christian's heart.

Fifth. The son that was pomised was a type of the promised Son of God.

Sixth. The offering of his son willingly was a type of the son that was offered in sacrafice for the sin of the world. How much is that type worth to this world?

Seventh. The typical family went into bondage, and all that went out were born in bondage; so the whole human race is born under the bondage of sin. The type is perfect and valuable.

Eighth. When the burden grows heavy and they crave for deliverance that is the convicted sinner.

Ninth. When the Lord sent Moses to bring them out of heathen bondage it is the sinner's conversion from darkness to light.

Tenth. When the blood of the lamb was sprinkled on the door and saved them it meant the atoning blood of Christ shed on Calvary.

Eleventh. Eating the passover was the type of eating the flesh and drinking the blood of Christ spiritually.

Twelfth. When they came to the Red Sea it is the type of the Christian, after conversion, coming into trouble, real or imaginary.

Thirteenth. When they cry to the Lord and trust the sea divides and they go on, the fittest type possible of the deliverance that Christians have received millions of times.

Fourteenth. When they see their enemies destroyed the type is just as strong, for the Christian that conquers in this first conflict never sees the same enemy again. These are the Lord's promises to his people by types, and the whole nation makes a type that is not capable of being misunderstood nor misconstrued if the type is seen. The New Testament gives us all these by words, but the words are preverted and their meaning utterly confouuded. Study the type and it cannot be confounded, and that is wherein they are so incalculably valuable.

Fifteenth. After they passed over the sea and saw their enemies overcome, they sang a song to the Lord, and gave thanks, and uttered praises and brought their worship to their great deliverer. This is the fittest type that could be shown of the Christian who seems to pass through extreme trials after his conversion, but trusts and finds himself safely through. He is filled with praises.

Sixteenth. The falling of the manna to sustain the physical man is perfect type of the spiritual nourishment of the Christian.

Seventeenth. The pillar of fire and the pillar of cloud to make the way plain and for their defense. The knowledge of these is more the matter of experience than the other types, so it seems to me.

Eighthteenth. The smiting the rock that Israel might drink, how fully it represents the water of life that sustains the Christian.

Nineteenth. When they came to Mt. Sinai and heard the commandments by the divine voice is this not a type of the Christian who has traveled the

Christian path till he feels the need of instruction? He opens the Lord's book of revelations and finds both law and gospel proclaimed, and from thence forth is subject to all the injunctions of the scripture except the ceremonial part which cannot literally apply to the Christian, but do apply in their types.

After that the man Moses was called up into the mountain to receive the tables of the law and instructions to build the tabernacle and all the typical things connected with it. The types of going into the mount, receiving the two tables, coming down and breaking them, and going back to obtain others. I am not sure that I see it all, but notice some of the plainer things.

The tabernacle represents the Christian physically. It was composed of not very strong or permanent material, was often moved about, and contained many items. It also represented the Christian mentally, being naturally dark and needing a constant supply of light. There was the golden candlestick with center shaft and six branches all the same height, and on them were seven sockets, each to hold a lamp. These seven lamps were trimmed and filled with the precious oils and lighted night and morning and were kept in the tabernale, burning constantly day and night. These lamps are types of the seven independent and essential attributes of the divine character, out of which every virtue and excellency proceed. The type is that these seven spirits of God Truth, Love, Power, Wisdom, Justice, Mercy and Immutability may, and should ever be, as brightly burning lamps in the heart and life of every Christian. When it is not so, then the person in whom it fails is just so far below his privilege, and also his duty. When these lamps are replenished, the oil or incense is burned on the golden altar, and kept constantly burning. That is the type of the constant spirit of worship, prayer and praise.

With these there is offered a lamb sacrafice. That represents the Lamb of Calvary. All there together is the divine authority for the high privilege of family worship, and it is so clearly defined that all the talent on earth cannot throw a cloud over it if the type is held fast. There is much more of this. But now, O man, Christian or infidel, civilized or savage, can the whole earth show stronger philosophy for anything? These types are the clearest conditions of the salvation or the condemnation of the human race. The authorship of the Bible is established stronger than anything can be established by the sworn testimony of man.

CHAPTER XII.

TRANSLATION.

In the foregoing chapters have been considered these points of difference between philosophy and orthodox theology, in which the two seem to be hopelessly irreconcilable; and also being shown those several points most important in theology which make the entire book of revelation harmonious, philosophical and clear.

The design will now be to compare the several chapters of this writing, with all the dark or difficult passages in the Bible, and show that the Bible is not dark, but that true theology and true philosophy are at perfect agreement with each other.

But have we any Bible? And if we have, then have we any reliable translation of it into the English language? As there have been, and are many translations, are there not some reasons, scriptural and logical, why one of these translations should be relied on to the exclusion of all the rest? If not, then we have nothing reliable. No reasoning can be wise if it has not a reliable foundation. But if we can find a solution of the disputed question that will show cause and effect on a fair line of reasoning until we find an authorized translation from the highest authority, then we may reason from it. The translation of A. D. 1611, called the King James translation, will show this logical claim to superiority. It was made by forty-seven men, of competent scholarship, and integrity of character, all acting under legal authority of the soverignty of the government. The very design of the whole thing was to obtain a true and faithful translation of the original copy of the Old and New Testaments into the English language. These translators were hired and paid by their king, not to give their own opinions any weight in the entire work, but that the translated Bible should be perfectly the same as was the original copies from which it was translated; and if the scholars of that age had detected defections in that work, the translators would have been liable to be called to an account for unfaithfulness in their work.

Another feature of this question is that the powers that be, are ordained of God, and King James the I, was not only ordained of God, but was as really under his control as any man that ever did contribute to the making up of the book of revelation, whether he was righteous or not. From these considerations we cannot reasonably regard the translation of A. D. 1611 as anything less than a God-given translation, and it should be counted valid and not a word of it changed.

In consideration of the vast number of the inhabitants of earth that use the English language, and of the probability of its use widening into other lands and becoming and remaining the most important language of the whole earth, nothing less than infidelity could doubt that the Lord did especially overrule the King James translation of the scriptures.

But the objectors come up with something of which they have just made the very valuable discovery; they have seen plainly that many words entering into narratives or paragraphs of the scripture and giving it special significance, should have been rendered in other words, for in the original, the rendering used is quite a remote one, the first and second significations having been omitted, and sometimes the fifth or tenth or some other one chosen. Any scholar can see that the first and plainest renderings have been passed by, and sometimes the most remote renderings, or nearly so, is inserted, and those objectors will triumphantly demand of the friend of our authorized version "What do you say to that?" Well, my answer is first, what do you think of yourself when you come to the front and do not seem to suppose that you are under any obligation to anyone, but you measure yourself up to those forty-seven translators and show without doubt that they are all wrong, and virtually say to the world and the church "Cast the rendering of those translators away as mistaken, incorrect and worthless, and take my rendering; I know more than all of them? True, they were under obligation to legal authority, and every text must undergo the closest scrutiny of the entire forty-seven, and receive the sanction of a majority, or, some say the sanction must be unanimous. But the advanced education of to-day shows that they are all wrong; I show you the clear truth in the case. My friend do you not feel a sense of shame at this point? My second answer is, the strength of the translation of A. D. 1611, lies in this: That the translations, which have been made by self-appointed committees under no legal obligation, would exhibit the prejudices of the translators, who would not study long about the first and plainst rendering of any word in the original but would insert the one having the most power in it, in a general sense, though perhaps very greatly to the confusion of the whole volume. If there were hundreds of the translators, and they were the best scholars in the world, the fact would only give them the stronger assurance in their self righteousness. But this committee of forty-seven men, under the authority of their legal soverign, who paid for their time, and required truth that would abide the inspection of all the future, such committee could not insert the first and plainest rendering without quite another qualification, which was as to whether it would make the sense of the original copy perfect in the translation. If the first will not, then will the second, or will the third, or will the fourth, or the tenth, or the fifteenth?

Like the prophet, Samuel, when he was sent to the house of Jesse to anoint a king, and all the sons who were present were brought before the prophet, all good looking, but all rejected. What will be done now? Why search till the right one is found, and though the shepherd boy was not so likely looking, yet he was the one taken.

In like manner, these forty-seven translators must find a rendering that would perfectly show the same meaning as that contained in the original copies and if they passed ninty and nine that would not make the perfect translation of the old into the new, reject them, and if one can be found perfectly fitting to the purpose required, take it, though it might be but little used, take it.

Another important item in favor of the translation of A. D. 1611 is, that it shows perfect harmony in every part of it with every other part of it, and the same harmony with all nature, but any change that would affect the meaning would make confusion. The reason a new translation is ever wanted is because people do not stop long enough in life's hurry to see the clearness of philosophy that is in and all through the Bible, as it is. This pamphlet must be proven to be in conflict with the Bible, or it must be acknowledged that the King James translation shows the brightest philosophy in the Bible, that there is in nature, but if that translation is moved at any point it will darken its brightness. In the light of that translation, the Bible shows the origin of all things, and a necessary reason why all things in nature are as they are, both the good and the bad, the past, the present and the future. It shows the necessity of letting sin reign in the earth as we see that it does, and has done, and also shows the indispensible necessity of future rewards and punishments. This philosophical clearness connects the entire Bible, and to disturb it at any one point, will disturb it in its relative proportion in all of its parts. It is clearly manifest that the very passages that men wish to have changed to show their idea of the Bible, plainly would do what they wish to have done, but it would introduce into the Bible a confusion that would be hopelessly irreconcilable. Neither the church nor the world can afford to have that translation touched. But another idea, not at all insignificant, is that it is the indispensible duty of the Christian people of the earth to try and prove and search until they find a translation that will prove true under the scrutiny of all ages, and all enemies. There is but one that is capable of enduring such an ordeal, and the authorized version will hold good in the light of reason, or testimony. But these assertions are made, and held only on the points of theology, and the general arrangement of this pamphlet. They cannot be held on the common orthodox theology. Our translation and the Bible that it translates are alike, all God given, and perfectly reliable.

But if this is to be a scrap chapter we introduce another thought somewhat different. In the foregoing item the word "theology" was applied to this pamphlet.

In view of the great amount of writing on theology by all denominations, if some one would see the term theology apblied to this writing, the reader might think that the writer was a full-fledged egotist.

But what is the meaning of the word theology? The religious denominations of the world put their denominational holdings into writing, as to the doctrines they require their members to acknowledge and support and the religious duties they are to observe.

Such a work is the theology of the people that issues the work. If they were all collected, and read by the same person, they would leave the reader where he could not successfully deny that there are real difficulties in parts of the Bible.

It has been the burden of my heart for years to see the book of life, the light of the world, the hope of the world, even the Bible, raised up from under this slander; and now I request, my orthodox brother or sister, or my infidel neighbor, that you scrutinize these twelve chapters closely in the light of truth and in the sight of a heart-searching judge, and then compare them with the Bible, and if the fair solution of the Bible will condemn this pamphlet, then let it be condemned. But if in the light of truth and scripture, and reason, the pamphlet cannot be condemned, then let the slander be removed, the infidel answered at every point, and the Bible be the most philosophical book on earth.

THE PHILOSOPHY OF PRAYER.

Prayer is philosophical as day and night. It is the petition of the spiritual soldier for army supplies. In all secular warfare all military supplies are furnished for the soldiers by the power they serve.

But the spiritual warfare is of more weighty importance than all the secular wars of the world from first to last, and the means adopted for supplying the spiritual army is that every soldier personally petition the commander for personal supplies and receive them. If the same thing is wanted by a number, let them all join the petition, whether together or separate, send up the verbal petition and receive what they ask, petition largely and receive largely and be strong and overcome. The secular soldier meets arms with the same kind of arms, but the spiritual soldier meets and must meet all visible arms that can be brought against him, not with visible arms, but with the spirit of his Commander, overcoming evil with good.

The very nature of the spiritual warfare is that the divine attributes are the arms of the spiritual, and in the hands of the soldier of the cross must overcome every principle or practice that is in opposition to them. If the soldier is hated, let him overcome it with love. If men abuse him, pray for them. Overcome evil with good, and wrong with right, and hatred with love. This requires a strength of character that the secular soldier has not the slightest conception of. It requires a firmness of purpose that puts its possessor above the world. These wants can only be supplied by petitions to the Commander for the needful supplies. These petitions, when properly presented, cannot fail to be complied with, and the want supplied, and the want to be supplied is so vastly more than the wants of the secular soldier can be. The philosophy of prayer is indisputable. The soldier of the cross is ready to be hated of all men for His name's sake, or to have his name cast out as evil, and suffer any kind of abuse, and rejoice that he is counted worthy to suffer shame for His name.

The political soldier receives his supplies through many hands, and by written communications. But if the spiritual soldier received his in that way he might and often would be cut off.

His Commander knows the whole situation, and

confers the supply to the petitioner directly. But these vast effects that the soldiers of the cross accomplish could not be reached if the soldiers would be careless and neglect to ask for their supplies.

Hence it is seen that prayer as a privilege is logical as any thing in nature.

A DEEP QUESTION.

How can justice be indemnified in the creation of men with a perfect knowledge of all the results of their creation, the knowledge that their existence should be endless, that they must endure the consequences of their probation, though short and uncertain, (as human life.) but after death holding them in existence everlastingly, and that if they die in sin they must remain in hopeless dispair of relief? Is not this irrevocable decree doctrine in its fullest force? No, it is not, for it does not depend on a decree, but upon a necessity in nature, that this world should accomplish the warfare for the annihilation of the power of the great enemy of the universe, and for securing peace and safety to all the Lord's vast empire throughout the endless future. It was the pre-requisite of creation.

Justice is indemnified again from the fact that the Creator furnished the agents with ample means of self defense so that they need not be hurt by the enemy except they chose to be. No more could be done for their defense without destroying their agency. But agency is a real necessity for man to accomplish the object for which the natural necessity required his existence.

A third indemnity is that there is, by a fixed law of nature, a principle inherent in agency the principles of happiness or of misery that depends on the agent. If memory and conscience, both deathless faculties of the soul, are burdened with guilt, it will be to the disembodied spirit like as fire and brimstone to the physical nature, (Bible teaching). But if these faculties of the spirit are found to be redeemed, pardoned, washed, pure and holy, and with a reconciled Savior, that will be heaven to them. It is then clear that these destinies depend on cause and effect, and the causes are all in the power of the agent alone, for the Creator has done all that the Creator could do to save every one who is an agent.

The Lord says, Ezekel xviii:32, "I have no pleasure in the death of him that dieth, saith the Lord God; wherefore turn yourselves and live." See verse 23, See chapter 33 and verse 11. And 1st Timothy ii:4; "Who will have all men to be saved, and to come to the knowledge of the truth." And 2d Peter iii:9, "Not willing that any should perish, but that all should come to repentance."

Our redeeming Lord could weep over Jerusalem like one who had made all provisions for the comfort of his family, but his children would reject his counsels and go off to the wilderness, and some froze to death, and others be found so frozen that their limbs must be amputated, and others perish with hunger. The parents could cry over them, and renew their counsels to them, but could not control them. The Almighty does not lack the power to control His creatures, but power is in debt to justice, for justice suffered the creation of all things on credit. Power made a decree that the enemy should be overcome, and its power destroyed so soon as created nature could be sufficiently developed to accomplish that vast work. Hence the Lord, even the Almighty, is under bonds to justice to finish that vastest work in nature, and to make it perfect. Sympathy and love are not dead toward sinners, but justice requires that they must be suffered to choose their course in life. They may be warned, admonished, induced, plead with, wept over, but justice forbids them to be coerced from their voluntary agency.

Closely allied to the above question and answer, is another question that has seemed to be dark to some people, and seemed strong in the hands of the infidel. That is, how can truth be indemnified in the offer of life and salvation to the entire human race, if the Creator knew from the beginning who would, and who would not, accept the offer of life and be saved? The answer is like unto the other answer in part, but in addition to that some other thoughts belong to this question, such as that the knowledge did not depend on any ruling of the Lord over the agent, for every one could and must make his own independent choice. Neither was it because the same provision was not made for those who are lost as there was for those who are saved. All were redeemed alike, and it was and is impossible that any could be lost who were not redeemed. The throne must appear perfect and unimpeachable. But the knowledge was the result of the infinity of the Divine nature, of His infinite wisdom and knowledge, His infinite perfection.

It is shown beyond cavil that the Lord possessed the most absolute power over all demons, snd they well knew that fact; but He suffered them to go on with their work and fill the world with influences favorable to seduce men into their service. The Lord used influences to induce men to righteousness, not to compel them, but to persuade them, that the enemy never could complain of a lack of facilities for the success of His cause, fully equal to those against Him.

But with truth and love, power and wisdom, justice and mercy, and immutability is the Lord's warfare carried to a successful issue, all showing that His purpose was not to prevent sin, but to overcome it. Now here is a solution of these dark questions that is scriptural and logical, reasonable and true, one that infidelity cannot move from the hands of Christianity, but the Christian can subdue the infidel with it on his own ground with his own weapon.

CHAPTER XIII.

TOPICS OF CHAPTERS AND REMARKS.

1. In the first chapter the first item shows testimony in nature to prove the existence of the God of the Bible, and it is proven to a demonstration.
2. The second item considers the attributes of the character of the God of the Bible, and proves it by the Bible.
3. The third item shows atonement decreed before creation and proves it by the Bible.
4. The fourth item shows that sin could not originate from creation, and is proven in proving the other items, as well as by such passages as these: "As I live saith the Lord God, I have no pleasure in the death of the wicked," and " Why will ye die?"
5. The fifth item shows the origin of sin was a principle in nature eternal as the attributes, and the combination of all these chapters establishes it, and revelation does not dispute, but does support it.
6. The sixth item shows the work of creation

barred until provisions were secured to bring that power of sin to a final end. These appropriations were the atonement, and a suitable race, and a suitable planet for the war against sin. Now when it is seen that there is not a hint in the Bible against this solution but a very great deal to support it. Then it is proven. The warfare commenced with the fall of man. There was enmity put between the serpent and the woman. "It shall bruise thy head, and thou shalt bruise his heel." But when Christ came, he says, "I beheld Satan as lightning falling from heaven." And again, "When a strong man armed keepeth his palace his goods are in peace: but when a stronger than he shall come upon him and overcome him, he taketh from him all his armour wherein he trusted, and divideth his spoils." "And thou hast ascended on high, thou hast led captivity captive." And also, "That through death he might destroy him that had the power of death, that is the devil." "And, having spoiled principalities and powers he made a show of them openly, triumphing over them in it." Scripture proof is abundant that the object of this world is a warfare.

7. The seventh item illustrates the warfare, and the necessity for everything that enters into it by the war of insurrection in the United States.

8. The eighth item asks the reason why infinite goodness suffers this world to sin so much and so long,

and many items of proof may be found for this. But the Creator being perfect in all his attributes, and the fact that we see the element of wickedness in the world, are all sufficient, and abundant proof that the world is doing the work that it was designed to do, and until it has closed its warfare, and finished the mission assigned it, the conflict must go on. But then will be an end of sin. Dan. ix:24.

The first chapter gives the elements of reason in many of the passages and parts that have been considered dark and mysterious, as why the atonement was decreed before creation, and it also shows the necessity of decreeing this planet, and the human race in connection with the atonement. The indemnity of the lamps required it.

Chapter II. But in the second chapter there is some light needful to be brought at some points, and the chapter shows that light, discriminating between creation and formation, and showing harmony in both. The chapter that illustrates creation is logically proven by scripture, and by reason and by all nature, and has its prominent place in showing clear, logical reason in all the Bible.

Chapter III treats of formation, and is a third link in the chain of clear logical reason in the entire book of revelation. It is clearly proven by its connection with first and second chapter, and the passages that treat of formation, and its relation to creation.

Chapter IV treats of the origin of sin, and shows a plain common sense solution of that hitherto dark and mysterious problem. Any theology that I have considered fails to show the divine attributes perfectly clear of any and all complicity with the authorship of sin. Both reason and revelation agree that even the omnipotent Creator could not do anything contrary to any one of these attributes. But this fourth chapter is self-evident truth and is a solution of all mysteries that were thought to be involved in it. It is in harmony with all the Bible, and strongly supported by many passages.

Chapter V treats of the fall, and shows philosophy and harmony in itself, and in all the Bible before it occurred. It is proven by scripture and philosophical reason and clearness.

Chapter VI treats of the warfare, showing it to be in perfect harmony with all nature, and revelation, and with the clearest philosophy and the experience of the world.

Chapter VII treats of the types of the old testament, showing them to be not only philosophical, but real necessities in nature, and to enter into the conditions decreed to be fulfilled, without which creation could not proceed. There were also other necessities, such as disciplining the Christian army. These types also show the pathway of the Christian in a way that cannot be turned aside by men's words.

These seven chapters show philosophical clearness on all dark points, from the first dawn of intelligence the Bible gives us, until the close of the old testament, and take all strong holds from infidelity.

Chapter VIII treats of gospel faith, and shows it to be philosophical as cause and effect in any topic in nature. The proof is, that it is so self evident that none who will look at it, can fail to see it. Another proof is that no word in scripture disputes it, and still another is that all the scripture supports it, as well as all nature.

Chapter IX treats of rewards and punishments showing the scripture to be perfectly philosophical, and that there also were necessities in nature, like all other things connected with the warfare of this earth.

These nine chapters set all the Bible in a clear, logical, reasonable light.

Chapter X treats of the design of revelation and brings to view a faint glimpse of the possible uses for which the Lord's book of revelation was designed, and the objects of wisdom and necessity that it may accomplish at all periods of the endless future.

Chapter XI treats of the authenticity of the scripture, a self-evident fact, clearly demonstrated by such a cloud of witnesses.

Chapter XII treats of the authorized translation of A. D. 1611, proving that we have a reliable translation, and that proves that we have a reliable Bible.

The word on theology shows that it is necessary to find harmony and reason in all the scriptures before theology can claim to be up to its reasonable necessities.

These twelve chapters involve a few general remarks or thoughts of a general character.

First. There is one self-existent being and only one.

Second. That self-existent personage possessed every attribute of character that is needful to accomplish all goodness to the fullest extent of the word, but didn't possess any attribute that was capable of doing wrong, and could not be the cause of wrong or evil.

Third. The origin and the producing cause of all sin, and all evil and wrong of every kind or character, was, and is, an uncreated principle in nature, not a person or being capable of voluntary action. Its natural tendency was and is its powers, it was and is the antagonist of all the goodness of the divine character, but inferior to that and could not be developed until creature life would exist. But an intelligent agent could not exist where that tendency or temptation toward wrong could not reach it. Hence the warfare for the utter extermination of that power.

Fourth. To make a perfect work in this warfare requires a vast amount of work that pure hands and pure hearts could not do, neither the Lord nor his soldiers. But the wicked of the world and their leader can do that kind of work and it will not hurt them, as when our Lord was betrayed, and when he was crucified, and when his soldiers conquered by a martyr's death.

Fifth. The called and chosen and faithful of the Lord are his soldiers and cannot seek their reward in this world, nor their rest, nor their honor, nor their wealth, nor their comfort, but like their Lord and commander, contend with spiritual weapons only until death is the crowning act of their warfare.

Sixth. No prophecy of the scripture is of any private interpretation, but it contains the elements within itself for its own philosophically, reasonable and unconquerable defense, and for putting the disputer to shame at every point.

No person can aspire up into that light and excellency of the Bible to which it is his privilege to aspire, until he sees it in its clear logical light; for until it is so understood it is held in weakness and dishonor.

Seventh. There is no ground for the apology that some make for being at ease in Zion while the heathen say, "Where is your God?" and defy them to show philosophy in the Bible. Ministers and laymen answer that if we could see the reason for all the Bible, we would be wise as its author and would not serve him. This is more monstrous than for a man to undertake to swim across the Pacific Ocean at the widest point, if he swim at all. But to acquire a logical knowledge of the Bible is but the threshold of Bible investigation, and the farther one investigates the more exhaustless the field of thought will appear.

Eighth. From the general tenor of these Bible interpretations it is fearful to consider the moral relation and condition of all the element of church as well as the world in the light of Bible teaching. Take from all church relation all that the Bible condems, worldliness and selfishness, pride and vanity, and how large a proportion remain? The Bible is all the light we have on that subject.

Ninth. These twelve chapters are a theological solution of all dark passages of the Bible, and from the interpretation these chapters make, any and all questions that can arise out of the dark parts of the Bible, find their philosophical definitions clear, logical, forcible answers.

Tenth. Any system of theology that leaves darkness and mystery in the Bible is imperfect and should be improved until no one would think of a dark revelation.

Enough has been said to make these pages plain to any person who might peruse them; for I am convinced that any subject may be made to seem dark by an extravagant amount of writing or argument concerning it. By this means the Bible appears to be the darkest book on earth, to the millions, to whom it should seem very full of light, and very easy to see its excellence at every point.

If these chapters will, on the closest scrutiny, be found to agree with all the Bible, and the Bible agree with all of them, then I cannot see why my task is not done. I now wish to commence at the first of the Bible and go through to the last of Revelation, and notice all the strongholds of infidelity, and compare them with these chapters, and attempt to show that there is not a dark passage in the Bible; nor is there a collision in it; nor a narrative that logical reason can spare; but there is just enough to make a work of philosophical, self-evident truth of divine origin so clearly reliable that the whole world may rest their salvation on its teachings, and meet all its enemies with arguments perfectly unconquerable.

Before we commence the comparison of these chapters with the Bible let one inquiry be suggested as to whether it is the privilege and the duty of the church and of the world, or of every individual, to investigate the Bible respecting its philosophical and logical clearness. Is it the duty of any accountable agent to submit to the investigation and interpretation of any man, or organization of men that ever did or ever can exist, and pass through life content with that which others give them concerning the account they must give to their final judge? I know there is a vast amount of teaching in various organizations that point in that direction. This kind of economy is the strength and the life of the church of Rome. It is fed to the children early as they can catch the ideas, and grows with their growth, and strengthens with their strength. This is their power and their tyranny, for it is conceded that the mass must every one prepare for himself his answer, when he shall give account of himself to God, and that it is the privilege as well as the duty of all who can read to do so, and to search for themselves, that would be the downfall, and utter ruin of the entire moral structure of this church, of its magnificent and costly cathedrals and of its imposing authority and tyranny.

A number of Protestant organizations occupy very similar ground, and seem to think it vastly extravagant to suggest that the scripture can be philosophically understood and logically explained. However pure the organization may be in its origin, nevertheless if it acquire popularity and wealth and power, and becomes numerous, yet still holds to the idea that the Bible is dark and mysterious, it will as naturally glide into speculation and tyranny as did the church of Rome.

Sometimes objections are set up against the investigation of the Bible in the light of reason, for they say men of great education and opportunities have said these vast topics are too deep for the human capacity to reason out. They refer to Deuteronomy, xxix:29, which reads thus: "The secret things belong to the Lord our God; but the things which are revealed belong to us and our children forever, that we may do all the words of this law."

Are the secret things here spoken of found in the book of Revelation, or has the Lord designed that the topics brought to view in the revelation he makes to the minds that he has ordained shouldn't be understood by those minds? Who could answer in the affirmative? But if that which the Bible reveals is that which belongs to us and our children, then what and where are the secret things if they are not found in the Bible? I answer, what is there in nature that the Bible does not reveal which is not a mystery? Who can fully solve the problem of sight, or of hearing, or of any of the five senses, or of the flower of the grass, or the grass, or the leaf of the forest, or a cup of water, or the grain of sand, or the bite of bread, or any other item in nature that the eye looks on, small or great? Hence what we have in the Bible is revealed and not past finding out; but that which the Bible has not revealed is mystery, and the number of those mysteries is utterly countless. But the scripture says, "Great is the mystery of Godliness." So it is; and the passage tells us in what respect it is great. But Godliness is not the Bible;

neither is it said the Bible is mystery. The Bible reveals why these mysterious things are so, and what they were for, and that is not any longer a mystery.

But the question is now with me, in the sight of the seacher of hearts, dare I publish these chapters in view of all the world, and the church holding that the Bible is not to be understood in a logical sense, or a philosophical light?

Infidelity has become so bold as to fill the principle cities from Boston to San Francisco with its poison, and challenge the whole earth to dispute its ground. In every case where the ministry has produced a written reply, infidelity has held the victory on their strong point, namely, that the Bible could not be defended in the light of reason.

I read a book with title of "Mistakes of Ingersoll," in which there were published about, I think, twenty-seven replies to his infidel lectures in Chicago. Some of these I thought were strong as could be made from orthodox ground, but the strong hold was not broken up, nor even tried. The next I heard of it, was in the fall of 1887, when Dr. Field, of New York, introduced a controversy with R. J. Ingersoll, and in many small points, like several others, he held complete victory over the infidel argument. But, like others, he did not meet the strong hold, and the advocate of the Bible stood second best. I could not but suppose that the infidel argument could not be met by orthodox theologians.

But I understood that the Rt. Hon. W. E. Gladstone, of British government notoriety, had published a criticism on the Field and Ingersoll discussion. I obtained the article and read it. I suppose I should read an article directly to the point, from a man of mind, not second to any man now living, and although I thought that a few others had made as good an effort as orthodox theology could make, yet Mr. Gladstone took a course somewhat different. I thought to take other good arguments with his, that they did about, if not entirely exhaust the argument that could be made from orthodox ground. But I found by reading the article that this mystery was most signally acknowledged. It was published in the North American Review of May, 1888. Pages 402 and 403 leave room to think the point conceded that a possible item of Christianity could be used as an argument against itself.

On page 484 he lends logical consistency to the defense of error; this should not be done. Page 491, no ground for assuming evolution and revelation to be at variance with each other. Now, in the eyes of most readers that will show his interpretation of the word evolution quite too near to Mr. Darwin's interpretation.

Page 495. He does not deny that the methods of

divine government present to us moral problems, insoluble to our understanding.

Pages 496 and 497. He acknowledges that belief should be defended only by such rules of investigation as common sense teaches in the common conduct of life, but then concedes the point that we have no right to demand demonstrative proofs, or the removal of all conflicting elements, either in the one sphere or the other. There are more notable words in this criticism but I forbear further notice.

In the ages when the Old Testament was written, the most of its meaning was dark to the people whose history it gives us. The very design of these Old Testament writings were to make types that should be light and law for all the future of earth's history, to make a perfect discipline for the army when the commander should take the field, and to perfect revelation, all of which it accomplished to the letter.

The people obeyed then without knowing why, but the Lord had demonstrated himself to them in so many ways, and so frequently, that the heavy penalties made them choose to obey, although they were blind to the reasons why.

But the antitype made his appearance and fulfilled the types, and completed his mission, and sent the comforter, the spirit of truth, purity and light. After that we read from Paul that the things that had been kept secret in the divine mind were now made known.

Eph. iii:9 and Col. i:26 and 2 Timothy i:10. When the apostle John was moved to write his epistles, in the first chapter he declares that God is light and in him is no darkness at all. All his word is light, and all his work is light, and all his designs touching the human race are now brought to light, and in him is no darkness at all.

With shrinking heart and trembling hand I write that it is my design to expose these thoughts in print to the public eyes in the name of the Lord.

The criticism of the Bible may be commenced by noticing the clearness of the testimony that the first three chapters of the Bible bear to the design for which the world and the human race were brought into existence, namely, for the warfare. The first three chapters of Genesis show the work of creation all very good.

The work of formation was good, and all continued good up to the third chapter and sixth verse, but in that verse is the account of the first act of disobedience, and then follows the immediate consequences of that act. For in that act man died, spiritually, and was no more very good, and the ground was cursed for man's sake, with all its productions, and the thoughts and imagination of man's heart as well. Chapter 6, verse 50. All the labor of His hands, and everything in the earth is brought under the power of wrong, by the first wrong act, which developed the enemy of the entire universe which is wrong as a principle. This seems the dark mystery of the developments of nature. But when the source of infinite goodness dwelt in boundless space alone, possessing all faculties for the production of all righteousness, yet not capable of wrong in any way, wisdom saw that wrong was possible, and possibility is the first condition of anything that does exist. But the onward movings of nature bring possibility into probability, and when these both exist then the movings of nature develops them into reality. Hence it is plain that possibility was the enemy in nature that must be overcome before anything could be created that it was possible to defile and ruin. Hence, infinite power put itself under bonds to justice that this possibility in nature to sin should be utterly overcome so soon as nature could be sufficiently developed for the accomplishment of that vast work.

But that work required the warfare, and the warfare required the commander and the atonement which the perfect God-head alone could make. Hence, the propriety and the absolute necessity that power should suffer the enemy to obtain possession of the entire theater of war that the subjugation might be complete, as shown in the chapters. In the scrutiny of the Bible the warfare will be the primary or leading thought, though subordinate thoughts will be brought out in some places, but all is considered subject to the one great object of the world's existence, which is the subjugation of the enemy, the warfare. The book of Revelation enters into the warfare and is a prominent part of the means used for the subjugation of the enemy, and to hold that enemy in perfect subjection everlastingly. All of this is shown in the introductory chapters, but this leading thought needs to be held in any and all parts of the scriptures. These views of the Bible show harmony, consistency and truth in the entire Bible, but to reject these views deprives it of all of them.

GENESIS.

Genesis i:1, "In the beginning God created the heaven and the earth. And the earth was without form and void." These expressions prove that the words "created" and "made," as used in the first chapter, did not nor could not convey the idea that formation was connected with creation. But as it is shown in chapters two and three of this writing, creation meant the legislation of the work and formation was the execution of the same work. The first chapter treats of legislation only, but nothing was brought into existence by virtue of creation, nor would anything exist until wisdom required it for useful design, and then it would be formed. It is neither certain nor likely that all that was created in the beginning had been formed or has an existence yet. If a new planet should be seen it was nevertheless created in the beginning. When the earth was formed, it was not without form, neither was it void. The same idea is embraced in the second chapter of Genesis, for it says the plants of the field were created, but had not been in the ground, nor had even grown, nor had there ever been rain upon the earth, and there was not a man to till the ground. Man had been created and woman at the same time, and they the last of all to be created, but there was not a man to till the ground.

Then we are informed of the first rain upon the earth, and the seventh verse shows that man was formed of the dust of the ground, and first after the earth, for there is no account of when the earth was formed, but it was ready for man when he was formed. But these things are proven in first and second chapters of this writing.

Since I lay down this writing, I read an article in a church paper. Both the church and the paper stand high for holiness. It seemed to admonish any and all against the teaching of so called philosophy, and there is a vast amount of room for that. But the article seemed to embrace the word "philosophy" entirely, and said, "The bread that man makes can not fill the hungry soul, but putting human fables under his feet, and resting in the grace, mercy and peace that flows from the Father through the Son." Now if the brightest and highest philosophy in nature was not found in all the Bible, and the very means of human salvation, then this remark might look better. But when will men cease to hurl the darkest slander against the pure, holy, divine character? For when the very clearest philosophy in nature is seen in all the Bible, and in everything that the Lord has done in, and with, and for this world, as revealed in the Bible, then the Bible will be the light and the hope of the world, and false philosophy will hide itself. But that is out of my course. Having considered creation as given in the first chapter of the Bible, and explained in the second chapter of this writing, a few remarks are presented on formation as it is found in the second chapter of Genesis and explained in the third chapter of this writing. Mention has been made of the earth as being without form and void after creation, and the words "formation" and "creation" defined, and also of all vegetables bringing fruit after their kind, before sun, or moon, or stars existed, which is a natural impossibility, as well as unscriptural. Mention was made of man and woman being created at the same time, and last of all things that were created, and that it is impossible in the very nature of things to reconcile the two chapters, if they are held to mean the same thing. Mention was made, too, of the second chapter, that the plants of the field, and the herbs of the field had been created, but had not been in the earth, and the herbs of the field had not grown, and there had not been rain upon the earth, and there was not a man to till the ground.

All of this is said after the account of creation had closed. As most of the second chapter was touched in treating of formation in the third chapter of this writing, but little more will be said here. But in the account of formation, verse 7, says: "And the Lord God formed man of the dust of the ground, and breathed into his nostrils the breath of life, and man became a living soul." The living soul was provided for man in creation, and in formation the entire race inherits it in the person of Adam, the first man. Then he planted a garden, and then out of the ground, made the Lord God to grow, every tree that is pleasant to the sight, and good for food, the tree of life also in the midst of the garden, and the tree of knowledge of good and evil. After telling of the waters of the garden, he put the man in the Garden of Eden to dress it and keep it. And the Lord God commanded the man, saying, "Of every tree of the garden thou mayest freely eat. But of the tree of knowledge of good and evil, thou shalt not eat of it, for in the day thou eatest thereof, thou shalt surely die." And after all this it is said, "It is not good that the man should be alone; I will make him a help-meet for him." "And out of the ground the Lord God formed every beast of the field, and every fowl of the air, and brought them to Adam to see what he would call them." Verse 21. And the Lord God caused a deep sleep to fall upon Adam, and he slept. And he took one of his ribs, and closed up the flesh instead thereof. And the rib which the Lord God had taken from man made he a woman and brought her to the man. And Adam said, this is bone of my bone, and flesh of my flesh. She shall be called woman because she was taken out of man. Therefore shall a man leave his father, and his mother, and shall cleave unto his wife, and they shall be one flesh. And they were both naked, the man and his wife, and were not ashamed." How different are the two chapters, creation and formation. That is most of the account of formation and it is in perfect agreement with the third chapter of this writing describing formation, or if not, let it be shown.

Now if this theology is strictly biblical then it is one with philosophy and removes all trouble or difficulty from these first two chapters of revelation.

Genesis III. This chapter treats of the fall of the first pair, and in them was the fall of the entire human race. As it is shown why and how in the fifth chapter it will not require a full investigation here.

But notice some items so brief, but containing such vastness and so clearly philosophical. The serpent was the tempting agent, but could not prevail of itself, but was met with an all-conquering weapon. For the woman's answer was "But of the fruit of the tree which is in the midst of the garden God hath said ye shall not eat of it, neither shall ye touch it, lest ye die." But the woman did not hear that command, for it was given to the man before she existed. But with that weapon valiantly handled all creation could not have produced her fall. And it settles a fact that all the earth is responsible for their acceptance of the Bible when it is shown to be reasonable, no matter who was the scribe that wrote it. And the serpent said unto the woman ye shall not surely die. For God doth know that in the day ye eat thereof then your eyes shall be opened, and ye shall be as gods, knowing good and evil. Here was the argument but no account of the woman yielding. But in in the sixth verse we see her scrutinizing the fruit and the tree. It is pleasant to look at, and it is good for food, and it will make us wise.

Now it was wrong to eat that fruit, and dangerous to be familar with it, for it was pleasant to the sight and to the taste, and will make us wise. Now it is plain that the agent was the tempter, but the wrong was the temptation. But they both eat of the fruit. And as they did eat thereof they both died according to the word of the Lord. When they were spiritually dead and physically alive they saw their nakedness, and felt a sense of shame.

There are a few things to notice in these parts of the narrative.

First, the weapon with which the Lord armed the woman, he has likewise put in the possession of every sane minded member of the human race, whether Christian or heathen, though they may not have heard of the Bible nor its author. That is conscience inherent in every human mind, and though some regard it so little, it might seem wanting, but it is part of their nature, nevertheless, and its dictates amount to a "God hath said," to them. But some persons listen to the voice of conscience which is the Lord's deputy and obey its dictates, and like those who were saved before the Bible was written, so they are saved.

Second item is: The tempter and the temptation seemed to gain a signal victory over the entire human race. But they were doing work that was absolutely necessary to be done for the utter and everlasting overthrow of themselves and everything connected with them; for the very express design of this planet, and the human race was to use them in their fallen relation. The warfare could not be accomplished on a pure and holy planet. As we look for philosophy in all this it is visible in every sentence. But look on a little further and see that the whole earth is fallen and become contaminated, and is in every particular fitted for a theater or war between right and wrong.

In Genesis, fourth chapter, there is an account of two murders; Cain slew Able and Lamech slew a young man.

The fifth chapter demonstrates that death is the lot of all, even the oldest.

In the sixth chapter is an account of the great wickedness of the world, and it is there said of man that every imagination of his heart was only evil continually, a true type of the unrenewed heart. It is also said, and it repented the Lord that he had made man on the earth, and it greived him at his heart. Herein have we the correct sense of the word repent. It means to change the course, to do differently. In this way the Lord did repent, for he destroyed man whom he had made. When one truly does repent of anything it is shown by his ceasing to practice that which was repented of. It is further said, "And it greived him at his heart." Some think these expressions clearly prove that the Lord did not know what would come to pass, until the sin occured. But this may be illustrated by the actions of men. It is said in some writings of the celebrated Napoleon Bonapart that on the occasion of one of his hard fought battles, when the interests of the day trembled on the decision of a few hours, there was a certain point in the heat of danger that required his presence. He moved for the spot with all speed, but on the way he saw one of his choice generals, one well beloved, who had received a mortal wound, and was in the death agony, but was still conscious. Their eyes met. Napoleon shed tears, but could not stop. He ordered a subordinate to take care of him. Quite too much interest gathered around that moment for the commanding general to heed anything else. He could cry for his friend, but must hasten away. His thoughts must be taken entirely away from him and given to the crisis that the hour had brought to view. In like manner the love and mercy of Him who commanded in the great fight against wrong was grieved at his heart at the sin and its dread consequences. But the necessity to make a perfect work required him to suffer the world to sin, just about as they did sin, until the ends of wisdom were met. Herein is seen the philosophy among all the philosophies, and that is the characteristic of the Bible.

Chapter seven. In this is narrated the details of the flood, and its consequences. But the reasons why the flood was sent upon the earth is given in chapter six, and the account all together makes the whole transaction clearly reasonable as any destruction of life in any political warfare of the world. The emeny's forces had gathered the whole race into its service, and was in constant warfare against the right and its author. The cause of wrong had possession of the theater of war and it must be wrested away or the cause of right would at least seem to be given up. But to suffer the enemy to triumph that far and then make such a display of divine power over it was a display of wisdom as well as power.

All nature conspires to prove indisputably that this planet and the human race were called into existence expressly for the great warfare in which the right must overcome the wrong, and annihilate its power to do mischief forever. There are few, if any, greater displays of divine wisdom and power in the entire warfare than is shown in the narrative of the flood. Neither the Bible nor the warfare could have been perfect without it, and it is philosophical as all the workings of nature around us.

That this world is a warfare is too self evident to be called in question, beside all the Bible teaching, and being created by infinite power and wisdom it is impossible but that the warfare was the design of its creation and existence.

It is equally clear that the Almighty does possess absolute power over all created nature, whether angels, men or demons. But the uncreated principle in nature, that wrong is possible, for that is the self existent principle, that is, and always was and always will be the antagonist of the Almighty. But that principle or possibility in nature is not the subject of command or control. But justice could not permit the creation of anything that could be corrupted until that principle or possibility to corrupt or defile would be virtually brought under divine control, and its power destroyed. Therein was the absolute necessity in nature for the warfare that is being accomplished in this world to destroy that possibility to defile or contaminate.

The only possible course to do that was to suffer it to be developed, met in warfare and overcome, and to make a show of it openly, so that all creatures would know the nature, and the wages of sin and that all creatures would be secured against sin everlastingly. Then it is clear that the whole transaction of the flood enters conspicuously into the warfare, and is to be regarded as a vast triumph, a signal victory.

But why make this vast demonstration at that special time, but never afterward? That is a matter of record very plain, for it has not been written since that time, that all flesh had corrupted his way. But the world in mass at that time had assumed a hostility toward their Creator that has always merited destruction and has always received it, as in the case of the Canaanites, and of the Sodomites. But it is written of the inhabitants of the earth at that time, "that every imagination of the thoughts of their hearts was only evil continually," verse 5, and verses 11 and 12, "The earth was corrupt before God, and the earth was filled with violence." And God looked upon the earth and behold it was corrupt; for all flesh had corrupted his way upon the earth.

Not only man was corrupt, but also the earth was corrupted by man and corrupt for man's sake Everything was fully ripe for a vast victory to be either gained or lost, but the wise commander of the forces of righteousness made it a notable success in the warfare, and made a revelation of this power over nature, and abhorance to sin and of the nature of sin to work destruction. But the war was not over yet, nor had the world accomplished its mission, and there was a remnant preserved to repeople the earth. The enemy was permitted to renew his vigilance until his work would accomplish its own destruction. Before leaving this subject let another thought be added, that is that in all cases where the destruction of a nation or a city or an army has been ordered, the reason for the order is easy to be seen in the warfare, where the people destroyed have taken such hostile ground in the war against the principles of righteousness that destruction was the only justifiable disposition to make of them.

The next signal destruction was Sodom and Gomorrah, and the next was Pharaoh and the Egyptian army in the Red Sea. Every principle of righteousness demanded their destruction as well as the interests of the warfare.

This next on record was the Midianites, emenies in

the war of right against wrong, with all the power they possessed. The principles that govern every secular warfare that has been successful must justify the destruction of the Midianites.

The next we find was those nations that inhabited the land that was promised to the twelve tribes for their inheirtance. The character of those nations did justify their destruction in the light of the spiritual warfare, and every feature of the transaction enters into the warfare, and shows real necessity to dispose of them as it was done.

Also the destruction of the Amelekites by Saul first king of Israel. In the light of war these were absolute necessities. Anything less than destruction in all these cases together with the cities of the plain, Sodom and Gomorrah, would have been a victory against rightousness. But the very design of this planet and the human race was, and is, that rightousness should overcome wrong in all its possible bearings, and make an end of its work everlastingly.

From the fact that the Almighty overrules all the wickedness that men and demons commit, and all committed against Himself, in the nature of things it is impossible that any wickedness of any kind could or would be permitted that does not in some way enter into the warfare; neither can any affliction, or trouble, or misfortune, or grief, or vexation. All the wrong that can be permitted or suffered to exist must contribute its part to make the warfare, or to hold its benefits in existence everlastingly. "It must needs be that offenses will come, but woe unto that man by whom the offense cometh." The enemy must be developed or else it could not be overcome. But woe unto any and all that choose to develop it.

After this they builded, and their language was confused, the world is divided, and Abram is brought to view, and in him the typical nation arises, in and by which Revelation is filled up, perfected, and finished. First, Abram was a true type of the Lord's true servants under Christ, whether laymen or ministers. For when the true heart sees clearly that the Lord has in any way given it directions, it is the meat and drink of its very spirit to obey, and there is no reserve, nor any exception to the rule. When God called Abram and told him to go into a strange land, He said to him, "I will bless them that bless thee, and curse him that curseth thee." This part of the promise is good to-day to every minister that the Lord has called to the work of the gospel. This treasure is also the inheritance of all persons that with their whole heart do follow the Lord as He invites and directs. The land of promise that was given to Abraham (name changed) by an everlasting covenant, for an everlasting possession, is the inheritance of every perfect-hearted Christian, but not in its type. We have not past the everlasting yet, nor are we his natural descent, but believers are his heirs according to the promise. In the typical land the heathens were to be put to death. (They were a type of the wickedness of the unrenewed heart.) The land must be cleansed perfectly, and a kingdom set up in which the Lord only is king. The perfect type of the Christian when all the old inhabitants, namely the appetites, passions, pride, malice, selfishness, worldliness, and the like are crucified and the pure spiritual kingdom set up in which none but Christ shall reign, that is the everlasting possession in its antitype, and the everlasting means endless.

In the fifteenth chapter a son is promised and he believed in the Lord and he counted it to him for righteousness, a type of gospel faith, not that faith had then or has yet either merit, or value, but when Abraham believed in the Lord it was with his undivided heart and that put all he was and all he had at the Lord's command. By his fully believing in the Lord, he was his perfect servant, without reserve, as seen when he obeyed the Lord when he told him to go into a strange land, not knowing whither he went, and also when he commanded him to make an offering of this same son that he inherited by his faith in the word of the Lord. His faith produced faithfulness in all his life and actions. That is the quality of faith that saves to-day and no other. It is not mysterious. This is treated in chapter 8. The Christian faith is as philosophical as the rising and the setting of the sun. God could not save sinners on any other condition and be just. Circumcision is a topic of the Bible, wise and necessary, and revelation could not be perfect without it, about as it is written, but that with all other scripture topics that in modest or refined circles would be immodest if brought into common use or conversation should not be brought into the pulpit or into religious conversation in presence of a promiscuous crowd or company. These topics were not designed to be used in the public audience, or in the social circle, but are necessary for private instruction. In this there is often seen a great display of depravity, for many men seem to choose that class of immodest topics that pertain to woman, or to sexualities and make the freest use of them in their sermons. The same persons would abstain from other topics of the Bible that are no more immodest than the ones they seem to delight in. But the Lord condemns adultery of the heart also. These displays often bring the Bible and the whole question of piety into ridicule and disgust before the world, and not infrequently to the disgust of the honest but weak inquirer, and embarrasses him in his search after Bible truth. If the man who does choke the spiritual infant to death by such inconsistencies, would murder the physical infant in a manner no more blameworthy, the legal authorities would prosecute him for the crime; but the human race may be murdered spiritually and no notice taken of it.

Passing to the narrative of Sodom, consider their wickedness, and filthiness into which the great enemy, wrong, had sunk them. How could created minds reach the conclusion that rational beings could, or would ever become sunk so deep into corruption as these Sodomites were found to be when these angels went among them, if the facts had not been developed and recorded where that work of the enemy could be seen forever? But the object of this world is to put the fruit of wrong in all its forms and magnitudes on exhibition, that the knowledge may never be lost. It is worthy of notice how Abraham criticises his Creator, but it is accepted and honored, for Abraham said to the Lord: "Shall not the Judge of all the earth do right?" These corrupt dens were destroyed, but the righteous were removed from the destruction. How much revelation is made in this narative of Sodom, and all philosophically clear. Genesis xix : 29-38 gives account of the incest in Lot's family, but not a word or hint of approbation can be gleaned from the narrative. But it reveals a few things, namely, that the power of wrong that was seen in nature before creation is everywhere, and again, these two children each produced a heathen nation that degenerated and developed character that became wicked, abandoned and finally lost. The clearest condemnation. The other naratives are Ebimelech forced to restore Abraham's wife, Isaac born, and the trial of Abraham's faith. What light this narative gives us: First to trust the Almighty in any and every possible case, and for the very logical reason that he knows all things and we do not, and further because he always brings more reward to those that faithfully trust him than the trusting costs them that do trust. But these are the smallest considerations. Vastly greater than that is that on or very near the spot where Abraham offered his son virtually to the Lord, there the Lord made a real offering of his Son for Abraham. By this very narrative the Lord has shown us what is our highest possible privilege, to inherit the wisdom of the Lord, which we may have if we trust perfectly and live faithfully, dark as it may seem to be.

The many short paragraphs that fill these pages do not require notice to reach our purpose, only those passages that seem dark.

In Genesis xxxvi : 31-39 is the record of the kings that reigned in the land of Edom before there reigned any kings over the children of Israel. Infidel writers speak of this as most conclusive evidence that the whole book is false for there were no kings reigned over Israel until hundreds of years after the death of Moses, and it is said that Moses wrote the book of

Genesis. They say that this was inserted here after the first king reigned over Israel. There are two logical answers to that objection. First, if Moses was the scribe that wrote Genesis, (but the Bible does not say he was,) he was not the author of any part of the Bible, and if he was the secretary that wrote, nevertheless the author knew as well all these things while the book of Genesis was being written as he knows now, and if it was wisest and best to order this passage written then and there, it would be so done. But if it was not the proper time to insert it, then it was not done, and it is not a shadow of difference whether it was inserted when the rest of Genesis was written, or inserted when the same passage was written in Chronicles. For the Bible could not have been logical at that passage if it had not been inserted in Genesis, because the Bible must all be so written that it will bear logical inspection.

Jacob and Esau were twin brothers, and were the subjects of prophecy before they were born, and Israel was Jacob, and Esau was Edom. Their connection must be traced to a certainty until the prophecy was fulfilled, for it was both possible and likely that two or more men of the same name would come into public notice at different times in the nation's history, hence the real necessity to identify Esau with Edom to a certainty while all were familiar with the history of the nation. But it is right just as we have it; all logical, plain, easy.

Now notice a succession of events, displays of divine wisdom, they cannot be less, in the governing this people, Israel, so that they do make the most perfect type of the life of a Christian, though Christianity was not introduced for twelve or fifteen hundred years afterward, at the same time filling up and completing the divine revelation. Commence with the conspiracy against Joseph who was sold, falsely accused and imprisoned, held two or three years, providentially brought out and promoted to the highest relation next to the king. Israel all went to Egypt, the fulfillment of the Lord's words to Abraham, but in the second generation they became the most perfect type of the whole human race. They are born under bondage to the Egyptians as all the earth is born under bondage to the fall and its consequences.

Here let one thought be inserted, namely, that the types that are so clearly shown in Abraham and his descendants from the time the Lord called him until the present time contain a display of infinite wisdom more grand and more exalted, and more clear and bright than there is to be found in any writing on earth. The same wisdom is seen in all his works, but in these types it is more minutely discribed and at greater length, and makes it so unmistakably plain. There are so many items, and they are of such incalculable importance and value, as, for example, that a political government could be, and was so administered as first, to answer all designs of government notwithstanding the ungovernable nature of the people that were governed; and second, that these government journals or records should make so perfect a revelation of its administrator, and third that these same records of that political power should at the same time make and show with perfect clearness and certainty the type of the Christian in every particular, both the affirmative, and the negative, though Christianity was not introduced for about two thousand years after the call of Abram.

In noticing these types it is not likely that they will all be seen, nor is it likely all is seen that is in some of them. But it is likely that enough will be seen to be a perfect light to the Christian path. If all who bear the name of Christian will hold the precepts of the New Testament in the light of these types it would determine to a certainty the meaning of those precepts, and show to an unerring certainty what is required to make the Christian acceptable to his Lord. And it would be the end of all essential difference of religious opinion, for the types are of such a nature that people cannot understand them differently, and that is their value. See chapter VII.

Exodus, chapter first. Inasmuch as infidel writers have made a very ridiculous showing of the people going down into Egypt, and of their coming out of Egypt, it is therefore necessary to show it up in a Bible light. The first chapter shows an increase of Israel altogether unusual; insomuch that it alarmed the Egyptians. But the infidel tells us that it was impossible for the number that went into Egypt to increase to the number that is represented to come out of it, in the time they were in Egypt, for they say there were seventy souls went into Egypt with Jacob. But the Bible counts by name the males that went with Jacob; his twelve sons and their sons and their grandsons make the seventy. See Genesis, 46th chapter. Mention is made of females, to show that all his blood descent went with him; but these were not counted in the seventy. Beside the seventy males, the twelve sons of Jacob had wives, and two of his grandsons, namely, Pharez, son of Judah, and Beriah, son of Asher, had two sons each. Now the females of Jacob's blood, we know not how many, and if these men had each one wife it would make fourteen more; if they had two to the man it would be twenty-eight more. But if they were like father Jacob, some or all of them raising families by four women to the man, it would be fifty-six women. Besides all that it was common and lawful to raise children by servants, as Abraham with Hagar, and Jacob with his wife's servants. Still further, from the accounts of those times and that people, there is room to suppose that there were as many servants as all the connection would need, so that all things considered in the light of the Bible and of common sense, it cannot be known how many souls went down into Egypt. It is more likely there were two hundred than that there were only seventy. If there were as many females as there were males of Jacob's blood descent, it would make one hundred and forty of his children and their children; and with other probabilities shown in these pages, the number that went down into Egypt could not reasonably be thought less than three hundred.

They say that Israel remained in Egypt two hundred and fifteen years, but the Bible says the stay of Israel in Egypt was four hundred and thirty years, and the self same day they came out.

Some of them, among whom is R. G. Ingersoll, take the statistics of our own early settlements as a standard of comparison. All right; I will show some figures from the standard history of the United States. Commencing with the settlement at Jamestown in 1607, we would have two hundred and seventy-three years until A. D. 1880, at which date the inhabitants of the United States numbered about fifty millions. From the settlement of Jamestown in 1607 to the year 1790, the records show the population to have increased to three millions nine hundred and twenty-nine thousand two hundred and fourteen; time, only one hundred and eighty-three years, twenty-two years less time than they want to allow Israel to have been in Egypt. Let shame burn the cheek of the man that will so designedly pervert the truth, and for no other purpose than to make a lie out of the only book in whose account the human race has hope.

Chapter II, Moses was born and taken care of on natural, visible principles, and yet it is miraculous as anything recorded in the Bible. Chapter III, Moses sent, or commanded to go to Pharoah. Chapter IV, origin of the miraculous rod. Chapter V. Moses and Aaron took the Lord's message to Pharoah to let the people go, and Pharoah said, "Who is the Lord that I should obey his voice to let Israel go? I know not the Lord, neither will I let Israel go." How plainly fallen nature is shown in that very expression and action, for the burden was laid heavier on Israel, insomuch that Israel complained to Moses and Aaron, and they complained to the Lord. And after these things were past, there is an account of the ten plagues that were sent on Egypt. Of these but little will be said, but they prove the Lord's power over all nature, to turn water to blood, or to call into existence frogs, or flies, or lice in any quantities, and cause them to do his will immediately, murrian among stock, or boil and blain among men, or hail, or locusts, or darkness, or death of all first born. These were not incidental things then, nor are they yet. We will notice the philosophy of these things with others of a similar kind, after a while. Does this show why men are afflicted so much because of disobedience? Chapter XII, there was a change of time that should last during the existence of the typical nation; and also the passover was instituted which should last as long. The Paschal lamb should be a male without blemish, of the first year. "And they shall take of the blood and strike on the two side posts and on the upper door post of the houses wherein they shall eat it. And they shall eat the flesh in that night roast with fire and unleavened bread, and with bitter herbs shall they eat it." A type of the atoning blood that saves the soul and that saved the body from the death of their first born. When one eats and drinks the body and blood of Christ spiritually, it must be natural, nothing feigned, nothing selfish, no leaven.

It was noticed that when those Israelttes who went into Egypt were dead, that those who were born in Egypt were the most perfect type of the human race, born under the bondage of sin. But when Israel felt their bondage to be a burden, that was a type of one who is awakened to a sense of his burden. When the Lord sent the man Moses to call them out of bondage, it points to the minister of the cross whom the Lord sends to call men out from the bondage of sin.

When the King refused to let them go, it was like the hold that the world has on the convicted sinner. The plagues show the divine care over any that cry to him for deliverance and shows the Lord's power over all nature, even the creeping things of earth. When they are brought out it is the clearest type that can be of the conversion of a sinner from darkness to light. But they slay the lamb and sprinkle its blood on the sides and top of the door, not on lower sill, but that very blood saves Israel, and the want of it slays the first born in all Egypt. When they eat the lamb with bitter herbs it is the Christian who eats the flesh of Christ spiritually, the bitter herbs being the bitterness of this world to the spirit of Christians. The Lord went before them in the pillar of fire by night and the pillar of cloud by day. These are known by experience to the Christian. Every true Christian knows the providence of the Lord leads him, but it is not seen by the enemies of the cross and of the Christian.

They come to the sea and their enemies pursue them. The Christian almost invariably meets with difficulties not long after conversion. They trust and wait till the sea is parted and the Christian will wait and trust but not go back until the way is opened to go on and find no harm. Israel saw the destruction of their enemies, and the Christian who fully trusts will have such a victory over his first vast enemy that he will likely never see it again.

The typical people hungered physically and the Lord sent them manna; it fell from above. The Christian hungers spiritually and is as really fed with the spiritual food that supports the spiritual life as Israel was fed with visible food to sustain the physical man. But can philosophy and theology marry at this point? If God is proven to be a philosophical demonstration outside of the Bible they can. See chapter 1.

This is the promise of the Lord to every Christian that while faithful he shall be sustained, and the promise was in the form of type that it could not be misunderstood. It was done by visible action, that is, example added to precept, for the same promise is given by words strong as they can be. This visible feeding of the typical people from the Lord's invisible store was a real necessity to make the correct revelation perfect in all its bearings, and where necessity is seen for anything its philosophy cannot be denied.

In chapter 17 the people want water and the Lord told Moses to take his rod and go. "Behold I will stand before thee there upon the rock in Horeb, and thou shalt smite the rock, and there shall come water out of it that the people may drink. And Moses did so in the sight of the elders of Israel." A like narrative is recorded in Numbers xx:8-11. Are they the same or are they different acts? But notice the types these narratives make. The people thirst physically and must have water or die, so is the spiritual man. But the water was furnished from *the* rock, not *a* rock. Here is the promise of the Lord by type, and the act visibly performed, to furnish the water of life for the thirsting spirit. The same promise is made by precept, or in words, but designing men pervert the word. The type cannot be perverted.

Now in the very nature and design of the Lord's revelation, it was a real necessity that this should be done, and put on record in revelation just as we have it, and that which is a necessity is philosophical. Our God of the Bible does not do unnecessary work. It was all literally fulfilled when Christ, the rock was smitten on Calvary, and on the day of Pentecost the water of life was poured out on all flesh. Let the disputer tell us that it is useless to eat bread or drink water to sustain physical nature, but let no man of brains say that these last two narratives are not philosophical necessities.

The next verse after the close of the supply of water is the commencement of another type, the war with Amalek. Now that narrative is filled with type, and lesson so important! Israel was the type of a Christian soon after conversion. Amalek was any person who attempted to turn aside the Christian while he is weak. The hands of Moses when held up enabled Israel to prevail, and when he let down his hands, Amalek prevailed. The hands held up means to the Christian when attacked by the world that fervent prayer to, and perfect reliance on Almighty God will enable him to prevail. But Moses' hands were held up till the going down of the sun and Israel prevailed. Young Christian, you need not be overcome. When the world attacks you hold up the hands. God is there. But the type that Amalek was to make is reserved to the proper time, and is seen in connection with the downfall of Saul, the first king of Israel, for his disobedience when he was sent to destroy Amalek. It will be noticed when we pass it, for it is utter extermination.

Chapter 20. Israel is at Mount Sinai and here the law proclaimed by a voice of terror that they do not forget while memory lasts, neither is its importance forgotten through time. It also has its typical significance, a very little of which will be noticed. The faithful convert to light and truth and their author, will hunger, spiritually, and will be fed, and will thirst for the water of life and it will be supplied. After he has passed through the sea in triumph and has had his sharp conflict with Amalek and conquered he begins to feel the want of instruction. Israel receives the law spoken to them by its author. But the Christian goes to the law as it is written and finds his rule of action in the gospel, and reads that love is the fulfilling of the law. Then if faithful, but not till then, is he prepared to do efficient service in the great war in which his redeeming Lord is commander. Now as to the philosophy of those plagues that were sent on Pharaoh, and other items that seem miraculous, if the great Almighty was acknowledged by the whole Hebrew nation to be their sole law giver for four hundred years and their nationality is as well authenticated as any nation that ever existed. These are the official acts that are recorded by the officials of the nation by order of their ruling power—not philosopical? If not what would you acknowledge to be philosophical? Is the celebrated Mr. Huxley one of the leading minds of the world for infidelity? There was published what professed to be an extract from his speech and in it was written as his words, "If there is anything in this world which I do firmly believe in, it is the universal validity of the law of causation. But that universality can not be proven by any amount of experience, let alone that which comes though the senses."

Then what could induce the belief in universal causation? Surely the book of nature only.

When nature is viewed it is seen to show design in every thing, and it is utterly impossible to find the designer other than the God of the Bible. But take a common sense view of all nature, and the philosophical and unbiased mind is driven to the conclusion that the God of the Bible is the root of all philosophy, the first principles of all causation. Then those plagues as well as all other miraculous things and all prophecy, are they philosophical or not? The introductory chapters prove that they are.

But in the tabernacle and the service rendered in it each feature shows a different type, the offering the morning and evening lamb, family worship morning and evening. Christians come in the name of and plead the merits of the Lamb of Calvary, a privilege and a treasure. The incense should be burned on the altar of incense evening and morning when the lamps were lighted, that is, family prayer. But the perpetual burning of incense is the perpetual spirit of prayer. The privilege of family worship goes back to the tabernacle. The seven lamps that were on the golden candlestick were trimmed filled with oil and lighted, morning and evening. It was kept constantly burning in the tabernacle for it was dark within. The human body is frail like the tabernacle, and these lamps are the seven spirits of God spoken of elsewhere. They also represent the seven essential attributes of the divine character, namely truth, love, power, wisdom, justice, mercy and immutability. By these typical lamps the vast privilege is offered to keep these pure lights burning in man's dark nature day and night, and the incense also constantly burning. O, why is this type set light by, or why not seek it at the cost of this whole world, if such would be required? The table of shew bread was holy. The Christian lives on the bread of life, which is Christ, but the minister's higher lot is to eat nothing else. His daily work is to study these things. These types when seen are so plain and forcible that they cannot be misunderstood.

The ark was very conspicious among the items that Moses was commanded to make. Was it not a type of the perfect Christian heart? It was composed of the choicest and costliest material. Its visible parts were gold, and the mercy seat of pure gold served as a lid for it. The cherubims were also of gold, of beaten work, on the two ends of the mercy seat. Within the ark were kept the table of the covenant, that is, the moral law. This represents the law written on true heart by the spirit of the Lord. It also contained a sample of miraculous food, the manna, and the pure heart holds in grateful memory the favors received of the Lord. It had within it Aaron's rod, that wonder working rod, whose motion seemed to bring deliverance to the Israelites so often, the emblems of their salvation by and through supernatural power, and the sanctified heart holds these blessings in memory. The Lord occupies the mercy seat, and the heart comes to the mercy seat to meet its Lord. The power of the Lord went with the ark, and the power of the Lord is found in the perfectly true heart. More might be said on the ark, but I do not claim to fully understand what the ark signifies to us. Another item of importance is the atonement that should be made once a year with the blood of a sacrificed beast for the whole nation by the high priest. This was a perfect type of our high priest when by his own blood he made an atonement for the whole world, the entire human race. All the sacrifices that were offered of beast or fowl found their fulfillment in the great sacrifice that our Lord made of himself to atone for sin. But after that it was not required of anyone to make a typical atonement.

NUMBERS.

Numbers XIII. The people at the wilderness of Paran pitch their tents and the command is given to send twelve men to Canaan to spy out the land. They went and returned and brought of the fruit, and when they made their report, two of the twelve said they would go up at once and possess the land, for the Lord had commanded them to go up and possess it, and the Lord would go before them and drive out the heathen. But the ten said they could not go for the people were stronger than they, and there were giants in the land. The people did not believe that the Lord would drive out the heathen, and would not go, and the Lord threatened them with destruction, which shows his justice in the case. But the man Moses ventured to plead for them, and they were spared. But we read the Lord swear in his wrath, they shall not enter into his rest.

All from twenty years and upward should not enter the land of Canaan except the two faithful ones that relied on the promise of the Lord. This type is of the highest importance. The land is a promise to the Christian who will take the Lord at his word believing his promise, and enter into the land of promise that he shall inherit perfect love, perfect peace, and perfect victory. They were directed to go into the land and possess it before crossing the Jordan, the emblem of death, for they were on the opposite side of the Dead Sea from the Jordan.

This type is a direction for the Christian and to the Christian how to obtain the perfect heart which is the antetype of Canaan, and is the fulfillment of the promise that was made to Abraham of an everlasting possession (Gensis xvii:8.) by an everlasting covenant, (Gensis xvii:13-19.)

When Christians reach sufficient experience to live in such a high state of bliss and not dishonor it, they may look at this very narrative and find the promise of the Lord that if they will go into perfect Christian liberty, and perfect love, and perfect peace, for this is the promised inheritance, the Lord will help them to cleanse the heart, as he helped Israel to drive the heathen out of the promised land. Give the entire will and desire into his hand.

But when Christians come to Paran and see that they may take possession of the perfect heart and live in the land of peace, which is to resign the entire will to the Lord in perfect trust, many of them fear to try, and seem to think they could not conquer their pride, or malice, or appetite, or love of the world, or of light, unholy company, or could not consent to be among a separate people from the world, and to utterly destroy all the old inhabitants and set up Christ's kingdom in their hearts in purity and truth. A very few go when they see the privilege, and live in a comparative heaven many years, and at last die in the highest enjoyment. But those who fear they can not conquer their own hearts and like Israel refuse to try, will most likely fall in the wilderness. But if they fight valiantly, holding up the hands (that is, prayer) until they come to the Jordan they may at last cross the stream into the land of promise. How clear is philosophy seen in all these types! The congregation are in the wilderness forty years until all the people were dead who refused to believe and enter in.

Numbers xvi:1–32. Korah, Dothan and Abiram, with certain of the children of Israel two hundred and fifty princes of the assembly, famous in the congregation, men of renown, attempted to usurp the preisthood to which the Lord had called Aaron, but the Lord caused the earth to be opened and to swallow up these three leading ones, and fire came out from the Lord and consumed the two hundred and fifty that offered incense. This type shows who may, and who may not assume the Christian ministry, just those whom the Lord calls and sends, and no other, though a vast number to-day bear the name of minister of the gospel, and thereby receive their support who are not called of the Lord to that work. All such may live and preach physically, but spiritually they are dead, and so are their supporters if they are not deceived.

Chapter xix. The water of separation, how it is prepared, and its use, is typical only. Many features enter into this type. There are many ways of becoming unclean spiritually. We may mention some, such as mingling with the world, hearing bad conversation, or seeing unrighteous actions, being tempted with unrighteous desires, inclinations or appetites, or keeping worldly company. Indeed Christians cannot live and mingle with and among the world and evade uncleanness. But little of this is real sin; but it is impurity and for it there is a fountain opened in the house of David, that is to the Christian spiritually, like unto the stream from the rock that was smitten by the rod, to Israel physically, and they stand in as much need of it as did Israel.

Now this type of cleansing with the water of separation is so full and plain that it cannot be misunderstood. It shows Christians's privilege to keep themselves pure. The species of uncleanness that requires the longest time to cleanse was caused by the touch of a dead body or being in the house where one was dead, or by touching a grave or a bone of one dead. Any of these would cause one to be unclean seven days, and he must not enter the tabernacle within that time without incurring the penalty of death, but with the proper use of cleansing typically, he might be clean the seventh day at even or evening. Now the dead body of the New Testament is the body of sin. That must be crucified and buried in the death of Christ, (Romans vi:3-4.) Nothing else will hide it and if it be never resurrected, it can never be touched. But if one incline to his old paths of sin, it is touching the dead body, and if he go to church before he is cleansed he would be spiritually dead while he is there. This type is designed for the benefit of Christians in general, and shows us at once both the purity and also the narrowness of the way of life and salvation from sin. But are the narratives of the earth swallowing up three and the fire from the earth consuming two hundred and fifty philosophical? And also the narrative of the water of separation and its use? All of these are the legislative and executive acts of the Hebrew government and that alone is sufficient to compel the affirmative answer they are philosophical.

Besides that it is shown in these pages that nature proves the God of the Bible to be a philosophical demonstration and that makes all his work philosophical. Theology and philosophy are not divorced in these items.

Chapter xx. Death of Miriam. The rock is smitten twice and the waters flow abundantly. Aaron dies on the mount. The Lord's chosen does not die in the valley of despair and doubt.

Chapter xxi. The type of the fiery serpents that bit and killed many of the people, and when they repented the Lord told Moses to make a serpent of brass and raise it on a pole, and when those who were bitten looked on it they were saved. This points the whole earth to the Son of Man lifted up for their salvation. Well, is that clearly philosophical? Who puts the question, and why not? Is not this pointing to the atonement, and does not the atonement fill all nature? And is it not the foundation of all existence and inseparably connected with all human life whether good or bad? And the type has so plain a design to show the real necessary condition of the well being of the entire human race. O, man is not this the clearest philosophy possible? If it is not, then pray tell us what is?

King Arad the Canaanite fought against Israel and

took some of them prisoners. But Isreal utterly destroyed them and their cities. Chapter 21. The Amorites subdued and the cities possessed, and by Og, King of Bashan with his people until there were none left alive, and they possessed the land. These with the Midianites, and people of Canaan, and the Amalekites were commanded to be exterminated. The first exterminated was King Arad who fought against Israel and took some of them prisoners. These were a type of the human agency that makes attemps to turn the Christian from his Christian life while he is young in the cause. But Israel asked the Lord for help, and received it, and utterly destroyed them and their cities.

Sihon, King of Ammon, refused to let Israel pass through their land, but gathered their forces and fought them, but Israel beat them and took possession of all their cities. Then Og, king of Bashan, withstood Israel, but Israel smote them until there was none left alive. These last two commenced the fight against the Lord in the person of Israel, which was a just cause for their extermination.

Here may be inserted a word on the relation these exterminating providences sustain to the warfare. In all wars of the world which are but types of the war between right and wrong, it is regarded as the duty of a commander to make the best use of the life of the enemy of which the commander is capable in order to reach the victory and accomplish the object of the war. But in this spiritual warfare in which the commander must reign till he hath put all enemies under his feet, the commander had power to exterminate all his enemies from the earth at a word, but he has use for them to bring their cause to the soldier of the cross that it may be overcome, for this warfare must be a perfect one.

Aside from the warfare in all these destructions there are reasons found within the narrative that are all-sufficient why they should be made. But viewed in the light of the warfare they are absolute necessities, all of them, for the enemy is overcome at all these points. Physical death inflicted for crime establishes the divine power and establishes the fact that individuals who involve themselves in similar crime do incur spiritual death in the very action. A signal victory was gained over the enemy in every case. In the first case man had corrupted the earth, and the penalty was physical death by water. The second was that men had corrupted a city (Sodom) and they suffered death by fire, and the third was that the Midianites had committed a terrible sin against Israel when they were the type of one converted from sin to righteousness, but not yet sanctified; they had not reached the type of perfect peace. The Midianites were exterminated by the sword.

The next to be considered were the seven nations

of Canaan and those two or three nations east of Jordan, all that inhabited the promised possession, the reason being shown else where. Put all these together and call it the fourth case of the kind.

The fifth case was the Amalekites, whose crime was an absolute demand for their extermination, for they had laid wait for Israel when they came up out of Egypt, the type of seeking in any way to attempt the overthrow of the young convert to Christianity. Now these sweeping exterminations were absolutely necessary victories in the warfare. Beside that the types they make all enter into the warfare, which was the sole object of this world's existence, and the sole object of the human race to make a perfect work of that warfare.

These remarks are sufficient for all the narratives of that kind, but the Bible entire enters into and makes up the warfare, every narrative its part.

But the necessity for their extermination was that they were in the land that should be the inheritance that was promised, for the two tribes and a half were legally settled on the wilderness side of Jordan. And the land must be perfectly cleansed of the old inhabitants, as the land on the Canaan side, and for the same reason which is treated in chapter seven. But notice a little more. The whole land of promise for the twelve tribes was a type of the human heart. The wicked inhabitants were the type of the unchanged heart. The perfect extermination of the heathen is a perfect type of the cleansing and the thorough change of heart necessary for the spiritual kingdom. But the entire new life, loyal, loving, faithful, was typical of setting up the kingdom in Canaan, after the heathen were put away, in which none but the great Almighty should reign. Now this new kingdom is the condition of salvation, but there are so few even in the church that do not deny this essential truth, though it is taught by words as plainly as words can teach it. But speculative professors cast a cloud over the plain words of the Lord so thick that many an honest inquirer finds difficulty to know the truth, but when these types are studied and seen they are so plain they cannot be misunderstood.

Is there philosophy in all of this? The very clearest in the world. These two and a half tribes that were legally settled on their inheritance on the wilderness side of Jordan have the promise fulfilled to them as verily as those in Canaan. That is the type of the perfect Christian heart and life and it is the Lord's promise to those who really seek that vast treasure that they shall find it.

Chapter xxv. Israel went with the heathen, and the heathen lead them into the depth of wickedness. They called Israel to the sacrifices of their gods, and four and twenty thousand of Israel fell because of the plague for their idolatry; "and the people did eat, and bowed down to their Gods. And Israel joined himself unto Baalpear, and the anger of the Lord was kindled against Israel."

But the 31st chapter records the judgment of the Midianites, and the judgments of these nations, physical or visible, is a type of spiritual punishment for a similar offence. To the Midianites it was extermination except the women children. This makes the type perfect in that case, for the women children when raised in and by another nation and becoming connected in the family relation with them, would never incline to the old ways of the nation of their fathers. But even this could not be authorized by law giver in cleansing any part of the land that fell to the lot of any of the twelve tribes of Israel, because the type that Israel would make should be a perfect description of, and guide to, the Christian life. And as the inhabitants that dwelt in Canaan were the perfect type of the wicked principles of the natural heart unrenewed, the command was to save alive nothing that breatheth. That means to those that choose the benefits of Christianity, to turn the world out of the heart perfectly, and keep the temple pure and the King will dwell and reign there. Now is not the salvation of the entire human race wrapt up in this type? But some would say, "We want that which looks philosophical." Oh, yes, certainly.

If the teacher teaches the young children to write by making copies of the letters or of marks without meaning, if it would instruct the pupils you would call the action philosophical, for the means are adopted to the accomplishment of the object. But this most important of all topics that concerns the work of man, and plain as the A, B, C, of any common school, that is not philosophical! Oh, shame!

But the design is not to touch all the Bible but only those parts that the disputers claim their victory on, or that the believers do not make plain, or both. Remove the darkness from those passages and all the rest will be plain.

But little more requires to be noticed until the crossing the Jordan, except the death of Moses. What an illustrious type is that! He is on the summit of Pisgah and from there he viewed the land that was the type of heaven. But when the soldiers of the cross calmly look death in the face with triumph and in sight of heaven, the very wise ones of this world say they are delirious. But this type is divine authority for the fact that the faithful follower of the risen Lord does often step from the mount of ecstasy into heaven and is not in sight of the Jordan.

But Joshua is commanded to cross the Jordan, the emblem of death, and enter the promised land. That land was a type of heaven, and also a type of the perfect Christian life on earth. The two and a half tribes to whom the lines fell on the wilderness side of the Jordan were a type in particular. For the wilderness side represents human life, and the tribes of Ruben and of Gad, and half the tribe of Manassah had the promise fulfilled to them as really as those who received their lots in Canaan, which makes the same type perfect that was proposed to Israel if they enter the land of promise from Paron, which they failed to do. But these two and a half tribes were the type of human life, and their inheritance was a type of the spirit and nature that is enjoyed in heaven perfect love, perfect peace and perfect victory, and the promise is confirmed to the Christian to-day, that he may inherit the principles of purity and acceptance in this life as really as he ever can after death.

The teachings on the more important subjects are often repeated over and over, again and again, as for instance, Israel being brought out of Egypt. Some infidels call it a boast to refer to it so often, but certainly it is not. Why should it be considered a boast? Oh, man that so speaks, to whom would the boast be made? Stop and think one moment in the light of common sense. When it is viewed as the type of bringing the soul from the bondage of sin into the light and liberty of the gospel, and the conversion of the soul, the change of heart from sin, darkness and despair, into light, truth and godliness, then it is not too frequently repeated. No, no, they are not repeated too often. Many persons of learning regard the oft repeating of these leading passages as the weakness of revelation. But after the laws of this world are changed from physical to spiritual, and the righteous and also the wicked of the earth gathered like the harvest and consigned to their eternal home, and this revelation so conspicuously exhibited that he who runs may read, and those passages that many fine scholars have thought to be illiterate or a boast are fully interpreted, they will see and say these very items are the wisdom of God. All could see them now we see the folly of disregarding them.

The topic most frequently referred to is the sacrifice of our Savior for the sin of the world. The type of the conversion of the soul that is brought out of Egyptian bondage is perhaps the next to it, and the perfect life in the world is nearly as often referred to.

To cross the Jordan was the type of physical death. It was crossed when in its most fearful form or condition, for it overflowed its banks when it was crossed. But the people who crossed that impassable looking stream do not represent the perfect Christian through life, who has walked the cast up way, always conquerer without a struggle. Such a one dies on the mountain top. But those who cross here represent those who have come through the wilderness and have struggled and fought hard all the way through and conquered, and they are at the river that represents death in its most frightful condition.

But the type goes on. After obedience to all orders, this terrible stream separates and the priests that bear the ark of the covenant of the Lord stood firm on dry ground in the midst of Jordan, and all the Israelites passed over on dry ground until all the people were passed clear over.

Now this is the promise of the Lord to the loyal Christian who fights through the wilderness and over comes. Such will get through death like Israel crossed the Jordan into the land of promise.

What about the philosophy of all this? Infinite power with a design so worthy and grand, ought to have done just the thing that was done and anything else could not have been philosophical.

But those that care not for the Lord and trust not in him find in that stream the death of all hope. and are soon in the dead sea in hopeless spiritual death.

Now these typical people are to set up a typical kingdom in which the God of Israel alone is king, as he had been since he took them under his special command and showed his rule so public, as in the case of the plagues in Egypt, and at the Red Sea and the war with Amalek and others, and at the crossing of Jordan. But now the kingdom hence forward is to be a local kingdom. The very design of this kingdom that Israel was to set up was to be a perfect type of the kingdom of Christ set up in the Christian's heart, and like the cast up way, must be so plain that fools should not err therein. Neither good nor bad could be deceived therein. The native inhabitants of Canaan were the fit type of the unchanged heart and life, and as in the type the visible inhabitants were to be perfectly cleared out of the land, even so under Christ, let every worldly principle be perfectly cleared out of the heart, and the spiritual kingdom set up in the heart, with nothing alive in that heart that could be offensive to the divine purity of the Lord. But notwithstanding the Lord's command to leave alive nothing that breatheth, yet they failed of perfect obedience, and they paid the penalty. In Jericho there was one exception, namely, the harlot Rahab. When the spies were there she believed and on her faith she acted, and hid the spies, and the good deed done on her faith justified the spies in giving her a promise of life for her and her house. On her faith was the promise, and on the promise she and her house perished not with them that believed not, but was brought out and saved. Now is there any mistake about this? Is it not the strongest promise that can be made to believing parents to pray and believe for their relations and receive them? The type that this woman makes is a most precious promise to the sorrowing heart, inciting to pray and not faint, to plead and not weary. Faithful father, mother, pray on! The next place to conquer was Ai, but what a terrible defeat.

All Israel fled before the people of Ai. Why did they fly before their enemies? Because one man had taken some gold and goods by theft and hid them. None in the army knew anything of it, except possibly his own family. But when the cause of their trouble was known how promptly they exterminated it; for they took the man and the silver and the gold and the garments, his sons and his daughters and his oxen and his asses and his sheep and his tent and all that he had and they stoned them with stones, and burned them with fire, and then buried them all together. After that they went up against the city of Ai and destroyed it utterly. Is not here to be found the reason why many people labor for a revival, but in vain? They have not put away the evil. Let all go into the battle with pure heart and clean hands. Put away the evil from among you! The inhabitants of Ai as well as of Jericho were utterly destroyed. Chapter ix—The Gibeonites by craft ohtained a league by which their lives were spared, but they were made to be servants. Chapter x records a narrative that is condemned by some as being unreasonable, unlikely and untrue; for the commander of Israel, when in an important battle against five kings, said, "Sun, stand thou still upon Gibeon, and thou moon in the valley of Ajalon " until the people had avenged themselves upon their enemies.

Is the Bible philosophical at these narratives, or would it not fail to be philosophical if these miraculous narratives were left out of it? It is proven in chapter 1, that all nature conspires to and does clearly demonstrate the God of the Bible philosophically, and the points of theology shown in these pages show the Bible to be philosophical up to this narrative. These types are necessary to settle beyond dispute the really necessary conditions of human salvation; that the spiritual kingdom of Christ must be set up and maintained in the heart. But this narrative shows by the type it makes, the importance of the kingdom being made perfect in the heart and everything worldly or selfish driven out. When Israel was in the battle with five kings this state of things was brought about expressly to show that the Lord does all things needful to reach the salvation of men, for in order that the type of cleansing the heart should be made perfect, the motion of the planets was revoked for the space of one day. It was within the power divine to accomplish in any way the destruction of their armies, but the necessity was to make this very type perfect. Why so? Because men were then and are now choosing their side of the army to fight, whether for the Lord or for the heathen. This choosing does not end with the warfare of this life, but the results of their choice are of endless duration. Love and mercy spare no expense to save them that harken to them. All is logical. That which is necessary to be done and is done is philosophical.

But those men who measure the power of the Lord by their own, say it would be impossible to interfere with this planet.

If the diminutive object that Mr. Darwin calls "monad" out of which he has evolved over and over, again and again, until he has brought all animal existence out of it, if one of those little creatures had seen one of that boy's marbles and would have said that there is no power that could handle this vast globe, even that would not be a fit figure of the man who says that there is no power in existence that can handle these vast planets.

The monad could be compared with a man and the marble could be compared with the earth, but the man can not be compared with the Almighty.

Being fully of the opinion that all Bible miracles are clearly proved to be philosophical they will not be noticed so much hereafter.

In Judges, chapter first, we are informed that nine of the tribes failed to drive out the heathen perfectly namely, Judah, Benjamin, Joseph, Manasseh, Epraim, Zebulon, Asher, Nephtali and Dan. Chapter second says an angel of the Lord came up from Gilgal to Bochim and said, "I made you to go up and out of

Egypt and have brought you into the land which I sware unto your fathers, and I said I will never break my covenant with you. And ye shall make no league with the inhabitants of this land; ye shall throw down their altars, but ye have not obeyed my voice. Why have ye done this? Wherefore I also said I will not drive them out from before you, but they shall be as thorns in your sides, and their gods shall be a snare unto you.

"And it came to pass when the angel of the Lord had spoken these words unto all the children of Israel that the people lifted up their voice and wept." In these verses there is a type whose teachings are of vast importance and concern to every person striving to reach his highest privilege in the Christian life. They had been frequently informed that if they did not drive out the heathen perfectly that the heathen would be an enemy to their success in their inheritance through life, and put them in peril of being hopelessly cast away. All this applies to every person who is about to establish a Christian life. All worldliness and selfishness must be turned out of the heart and the land possessed. If there is but a very little of self or the world remaining, that little will make war against you through life, and will keep you in the most iminent danger of falling in the wilderness or meeting death unprepared and never reaching the land of promise.

But the type went further. These people soon saw the consequences of their failure displayed, and how repeatedly it occurred, and how long it continued, and how great the extent of the damage they sustained by it. Ten of the tribes revolted from the king and set up another kingdom, leaving but two tribes loyal to the legal ruler. The ten ran into idolatry and all manner of corruption, as the heathen led them, until they were cast out into hopeless exile and were blotted out as a nation. Judah was carried away into a strange land for seventy years, and all their pleasant things were laid waste. They endured that calamity and distress for the very sins into which these heathen led them. All this is a message to the Christian to-day, and through all the history of the church. These types make a clear revelation of the Lord's will and rulings, and of His righteous judgment, and His impartial treatment of all men on the subject of idolatry.

Soon after the land was divided and all of them settled in their inheritance, we read that the children of Israel did evil in the sight of the Lord, and involved themselves in deep trouble. The Lord raised up judges for their deliverance, but they would not hear the judges, but intermarried with the heathen and served their gods. Therefore the Lord sold them for eight years, and when they cried to the Lord He raised up deliverance and the land had rest forty years. They sinned a second time but repented and cried to the Lord for help and again were delivered. And so it was the third time and the fourth time, and the fifth, and the sixth, and seventh times until the Lord remembered their ingratitude, and refused to help them so visibly as before, though he did not forsake them but sent different ones at different times to rescue them. But the heathen principles prevailed until every man did that which was right in his own eyes.

There's nothing in the book of Ruth to demand attention, but come to First Samuel. Here the Lord raised up the prophet, Samuel. The first message he bears from the Lord was to Eli the priest, and to his sons who were the priests of the temple. They were wicked and the message said the reason why they should be destroyed was because his sons made themselves vile and he restrained them not. Now Israel was warring with the Philistines, and they were smitten before the Philistines with the loss of four thousand men. Then the elders of Israel said, "Let us fetch the Ark of the covenant of the Lord out of Shilo unto us, that when it cometh among us it may save us out of the hands of our enemies." Now the ark belonged to the Lord and was of high importance. When it was among the Lord's people by His authority it was a signal blessing to them. But when the heathen captured it and thought it a great victory, it was a terrible scourge to them. But these wicked priests that were doomed to death, assumed the authority to bring it among them, and when the ark was brought into the camp of Israel without leave or command of its owner, then all Israel shouted with a great shout. They were excited at seeing the ark brought in a sinful manner into a forbidden place, so they uttered this shout of their own will. Their hearts belonged to the Lord, whether wicked or righteous, and an acceptable shout is only produced by the spirit of the Lord, but their shout was their own. Mark the result! The shout alarmed their enemies and quickened them to the deeds of those fighting with desperation. Israel was smitten and the two wicked priests, Phinehas and Hophni, the sons of Eli, were slain.

When the word came to Eli that Israel was smitten, and his sons were dead, and the enemy had taken the ark of the Lord, he fell from his seat, broke his neck and died. And when his daugher-in-law heard that the ark of the Lord was taken, and that her father-in-law and her husband were dead, the news produced her death also. Now here is lesson by type that shows how fathers should treat their wilfully wicked children. If the father has given them any public charge or interest, and they will not be faithful in that charge nor be admonished, let them be removed and put a faithful man in their place. It also teaches the necessity for men to keep their own heart with all diligence, and to distinguish between the will of the Lord and the will of their disloyal children, and it is a signal warning never to make speculation or self indulgence of either the house or the work of the Lord, nor hold the will of their children to the least extent in the way of their duty to their Lord. At Jericho when the Lord's messenger bade the people shout, then the shout had power, and the walls that defended heathen Jericho against the Lord fell without the aid of human hands. But though the ark was taken by the enemies of the Lord and the enemies of Israel, and they thought they had gained a great advantage in the possession of the ark, and brought it into the house of their idols and set it by Dagon, their idol, yet in the first night Dagon had fallen upon his face to the earth before the ark of the Lord.

They set him in his place again, but the next morning they found him fallen to the ground before the ark with hands broken off, and only the stump of Dagon left to him. But their trouble did not stop here, for they were smitten with very strange and sore plagues and very many died, insomuch that the Philistines were vastly more anxious to get the ark from among them than they had been to obtain possession of it. Whatever the ark may have been a type of, it was of so high importance and so essential was the necessity to make it perfect that when the men of Bethshemesh looked into the ark the Lord smote of the people fifty thousand three score and ten men. Verily, what does the ark mean to us? Is it the sanctified heart of the Christian? What else in the Christian church does the Lord set so much store by?

After these things the people want a king to rule over them, though Joshua had made and ratified a covenant with them, that they would serve the Lord as their ruler and no other. Joshua, xxiv: 26-28.

Samuel remonstrates with them against their demand for a king, but they say, "Nay, but we will have a king over us." Verily is not this world accomplishing the work for which it was designed in its creation before it was called into existence? For we see men choosing their own ways. The Lord shows right and keeps it before their minds, but they choose the way of wrong, and the Lord suffers men to do their pleasure, so far as wisdom sees a profitable use for their action to accomplish the ends of wisdom. "Surely the wrath of man shall praise thee, the remainder of wrath shalt thou restrain." Ps. 76 and 10. Do not these things prove that whatever wrong is not restrained, there is some influence in nature that will present it to the minds of men and they will do it? Strange that Israel should want a king, but the type shows us that men of perfect liberty under Christ will choose bondage to the world, and the bondage is more severe than the Israelites had it under King Saul. But the request is granted, and the king comes into power, and there are many things in his reign that are good and profitable. But in his history there are many things that make their special revelation clear and very profitable to the human race. For although to him was given a new heart (1 Samuel, x: 9) he offered a burnt offering (1 Samuel, xiii) for which Samuel reproves him sharply and tells him the kingdom shall not continue with him.

When the Lord tried him he failed to believe and trust. All men are tried and some prove faithful. But Saul seemed to be firm in his integrity, and so immoveable that he would have put his son Jonathan to death had not the people rescued him. But he disobeyed the Lord when commanded by the prophet to go and smite Amalek, and slay both man and woman, infant and suckling, ox and sheep, camel and ass, because righteousness required it, for Amalek fought with Israel soon after they came out of bondage, and was a type of the Christian lately converted. The physical destruction of Amalek must be made a perfect type of the spiritual judgment of anyone that attempts to turn lately converted Christians from the path of truth and righteousness when they are aiming to pursue the Christian life until they come to Christian perfection.

The type shows Christians that their only safty is to utterly put from them anything or any person that would tempt them to commit sin or do wrong if it is the right hand or the right eye.

But Saul was sent on a message and to perform a work of vast importance. It was not the life of a son that was to be either spared or sacrificed then, but it was the heathen king, and the cattle and sheep and something in the form of wealth. Obedience was better then than sacrifice. Now it is plain that such a king as Saul was a necessity to make revelation by such a life and such a reign, and by such actions as a righteous king could not do because of contamination, but it did not hurt Saul, for evil was his choice. But his history enters into revelation and makes it perfect and clear where nothing else would. In the history of Saul there is one very special and very important truth set forth. That is, no person living can be safe if he does not raise his Christian standard above all sin, for if any wrong remains not cast out it will be developed into condemning error.

Another thought is that such may be placed where he can do needful work willingly that a righteous man could not do, but do himself no harm. "The wicked is thy sword."

Is all this philosophical where cause and effect and necessity are seen, and each of them in its proper place? Are not these the very elements of philosophy?

David comes to the throne. It may be observed that the Lord makes revelation out of almost every step of David's life, for he is the shepherd boy and seems like a cast off, with the older ones all near by when the prophet went among them to anoint a king. But after all appeared all were refused, yet when the shepherd boy was brought he was anointed to be the king of Israel. Soon after his anointing he was unexpectedly brought before the king and more mysterously meets and slays the giant and then is very mysteriously preserved from the malice of Saul who sought his life. That is the Lord's care over his faithful servant, for it is observable that David asked the Lord before undertaking any important enterprise, and his success in battle is noteworthy. The Lord rules it all, and though Saul and David are spoken of as kings, yet they both acknowledged the Lord as their authority, and wisdom, and power and that he only had ability to rule, although David was one of the most distinguished men of all the earth.

The endless throne of him that inhabiteth eternity even that is called the throne of David, and the man in whom dwelt all the fulness of the God head bodily is called the Son of David. The Almighty says that David is a man after his own heart. What higher dignity could gather round the name and memory of a man?

But there is another development made in the life of king David, for to him is recorded a crime, and is it not the blackest on record? Surely to take it in all its bearings it is as dark as any, if not the darkest page of the world's history. But how could revelation be perfect and complete without this very narrative of King David's dealing with Uriah and his wife? There are so many items of weight revealed in this dark account, but a few only will be noticed. First, it proves clearly that no created being could withstand the seductive and tempting power that is every where, and did always exist, and is ever ready to occupy any and all ground for evil, when not restrained by the Almighty's power, whether it was the angels that first fell, or the first pair of the human race, or whether it was the king of Israel that was guarded by experience and revelations and such favored circumstances as was King David.

The second thing to notice is that if the very blackest of sins, the greatest of crimes had not been committed and pardoned then many persons might suppose that their sin or crime was so aggravated that the atonement could not reach it. But with this revelation, the convicted murderer, adulterer, imposter, or deceiver, if he repent of his wickedness, need not despair, but see that in the atonement there is merit by which he may be made clean, and if such should be lost, this revelation will eternally stand before him saying, "Ye need not have been lost, and the throne will be eternally guiltless."

A third item to notice is that all men belong to the Lord by a supreme right, and were brought into existence to fill some place, to answer some purpose, and if the Uriah's that are imposed on are wicked of choice they are only fit to make some profitable example in some way. But the man that sins against them must bear the penalty.

If they are the servants of the Lord and He suffers imposition to come to them then the Lord is their great reward, more to them than all their loss, even though they might have owned the world and sacrificed it. Think of the Nazarine! Another thought is, that sin is punished in the person that commits it, either on the throne or in the prison. Think of the punishment that so soon followed to the perpetrator of so dark a deed! His son dishonors his daughter, and another son murders the guilty one. The murderer raised and led an insurrection against his father, the king, and how the king flees for his life before his own son! That same loved son of the king dishonored the king's house in a way, and to an extent that the earth has not its parallel on record. And at the last, the death of his son who was pursuing him for his life, how it did bleed his heart! But this whole account shows that the Lord will bring good out of evil, always does. This narrative is of incalculable value.

1st Kings, i:5-49. Adonijah usurped the kingdom, and seemed to have gained possession of sufficient power and interest to hold it, and doubtless expected to take possession of the throne soon, because the king was old and helpless. Now, to what power can we attribute this turn of affairs? Only that the Lord overruled it, because He had chosen Solomon both to reign and to do a much greater work than to reign over Israel. As Solomon was so distinguished a personage, it is proper to consider what is taught by the type that his history contains. Was he a faint figure of the great Architect of the universe, and also of the great ruler? First, in his wisdom, and in his work, and also in his greatness, inflicting death on certain ones as a ruler, and deciding between the two mothers as to who shall have the living child. As an architect, or a deviser and designer, his wisdom is displayed in building the temple and the other buildings, residence, court, throne, and the like. The temple as a type, points to the spiritual church under Christ, or the spiritual temple that is being built of the material prepared in this world, like the rocks were prepared in the quarry for the typical temple, wherein was the precious corner stone or the type of it. For it was the true worship, but was a type of the temple of the heart where the kingdom is set up, in which none but Christ shall reign. And as the typical temple was built of stones that were perfectly prepared for the place they should fill before leaving the quarry, even so the spiritual temple that is being, or will be built out of the inhabitants of this earth must be perfectly prepared to fill and fit the place designed for them, before leaving this world. And as the temple is made of the most costly material, so must its antitype be, the material is the saved ones of this world, and is the price of hallowed blood, and is the most precious treasure that the Lord will gather from this earth. As the temple was the most costly, the richest, and in every way the most splendid building that ever did or that ever will grace this earth, even so must and will the spiritual temple be in all the vast empire of the universe. Then who has not underestimated his high and holy calling? But the temple of the Christian heart must not be contaminated with buyers and sellers and money changers, nor with the seats of them that sell doves, but these must be all driven out. But much more is contained in the history of Solomon, for he, being the wisest man, and having the most extensive experience, and also writing under inspiration, his writing comes to us by divine authority, and with double weight, and settles some questions beyond doubt; such as, that the life that fears and serves the Lord with a perfect heart is the happiest life that can be enjoyed, and is secure in the end.

The monster question, polygamy, is by divine authority settled in the person and history of Solomon, for he chose from all the women of the earth until he had one thousand women, and after all this experience that the Lord gave him for this very purpose, he says, and it is under inspiration, " Rejoice with the wife of thy youth." Not the plural, but the singular number. Proverbs 5:18; also Eccl. ix:9. "Live joyfully with the wife that thou lovest all the days of thy life." If there is more than one wife, none is loved really, and in the nature of things it is impossible for man or woman to live joyfully in the marriage relation if they have more than one companion.

The Lord said to the first pair "The two shall be one flesh," but with Solomon's unequalled advantage he loved and married many strange women. The heathen, then were the sinful principles of the human heart now. For Solomon to love and marry a strange woman then was the same as for a Christian to love and accept in any way anything that is not in harmony with true godliness, or to acknowledge or practice or indulge in it; such as pride, malice, hatred or bitterness, or love of the world or the spirit or the ways of the world. As the Lord instructed to sever all relation and connection with the heathen, and not admit their presence, but drive them out of the land, so that very command is an obligation to all Christians to-day, to shut every wrong principle out of the heart, with all evil inclination or disposition, and for the same reason that the heathen should be shut out of the land and from the society of Israel. In both cases they would lead the Lord's people into sin; and surely Solomon was an example of it, for that mighty man was led or inclined by these heathen women into the most aggravated forms of idolatry. He built places for the worship of idols, and offered sacrifices to the idol gods of these women, until the Lord rent the kingdom from his house, and it was never restored. Just so the kingdom of Christ is rent from the Christian heart in this our day, when they indulge in any way in the spirit of the world and its ways, and look with desire on worldly things. Here is the clearest teaching that can be on anything, that though a Christian minister aspire to the highest degree of usefulness even to call their thousands from darkness to light, yet if they willfully allow themselves to run into sin, or wrong principle, it is ruin to them. The greatness of these great men was not of themselves, but of the Lord, and they owe to him all they are, and all they have, just as much and as perfectly as do the minds that are of a hundred fold less magnitude owe all they have and are. Many think if their salvation requires them to give to the Lord all they have and all they are, the price is too high. Many choose the world rather than the obligations of a Christian life. They do not see that the only perfect liberty in nature is inseparably connected with the Christian life. The great men of the world are not brought on exhibition for their own personal interest, nor for the sake of those who are benefited by them, but that the world shall accomplish the object for which it was created, that the right should meet wrong and conquer it in all its forms and magnitudes. When the Lord wants a king David he sends a messenger for the shepherd boy, and trains him for the kingdom. If he wants a Lincoln to hold the reins of a republic, or a Grant to command the army, he calls them out of obscurity, and puts them in the highest places in the nation. The Lord's work will surely accomplish the object for which he designed it, to make his revelation perfect, and to utterly subdue sin in all its bearings and make an endless exhibition of it and its consequences. Surely here is the most logical explanation of these parts of the old Bible. Its types were all real necessities as well as harmonious and plain.

When Rehoboam succeeded Solomom, his father, to the throne, the promise to rend the kingdom was soon fulfilled, for ten tribes under Jeroboam set up an independent kingdom at Samaria. Soon after they made two golden idols and called them gods. They were made in the likeness of calves, and said, "Behold thy gods, O Israel, that brought thee up out of the land of Egypt." And Jeroboam made altars for the worship of these calves, or calf gods, and brought offerings upon these altars.

In all this we see that the Lord suffers men to sin just so far as a wise and profitable use can be made of the sin, and no further; and when a king, or nation, or both, choose the path of delusion, the Lord will choose what delusion they shall have that he may bring the reward of their delusion upon them, Isaiah lxvi:4. But Israel chose to divide and make two kingdoms, and the Lord suffered them to do so because they taught lessons by type that they could not have taught if they had not divided. The Lord does not call on men to do evil that good may come, but on men that are willing to be the dupes of evil. The evil principle will always occupy all ground for evil that is not restrained, and it belongs to the very nature of an agent to choose, and those that choose the wrong, if the Lord chooses the wrong that they may do that it may be overruled for good and restrains all else. Surely it is a wise ruling and injures no one, but the wickedness shall contribute to its own distruction. But the atonement is for all whether they are saved or lost, for it is impossible for the Lord to cast off one of His creatures for a sin over which they had no agency, and be just. Therefore the blackness of crime and all sin is the more monstrous because the atoning blood brought the pardon which is disdained. In the thirteenth chapter of first Kings is a narrative in which there are several typical lessons. The Lord sent a man to Bethel to king Jeroboam, to pronounce the fate of their idol altar, but when he had spoken the words of his message the king stretched forth his hand from the altar saying, "Lay hold on him." But the hand was dried up that he could not full it again to him, and the sign was fulfilled that the prophet had given to the king. The king, that the moment before had said, "Lay hold on him," now requests the prophet to entreat the Lord for him, that his hand might be restored. The prophet did so, and it was restored. Then the king invited the prophet to go with him and be refreshed, but the prophet said his orders were not to eat or drink in Bethel, nor to return by the road he came. All this looks like the man was a true and acceptable messenger of the Lord. But on his way homeward an old prophet of Bethel overtook him and said that he also was a prophet and that an angel had told him to bring that prophet back to Bethel to eat bread and drink water. The prophet disobeyed the order that he had from the mouth of the Lord and went back and did eat and drink. Then the prophet that brought him back told him that for his disobedience to the Lord he should not come into the sepulchre of his fathers. When the prophet attempted a second time to return home a lion slew him.

This type is the promise of the Lord to any messengers that he may send, under Christian rule, with any message, whether in Christian or heathen lands, that the Lord will go with them, and whether they meet life or death the very wisest and best results will be met. Another idea is, that the Bible is the Lord's orders to man under Christ, and when we see what the Bible says to us, let not the word or influence of flesh and blood come between us and what the Lord hath said to us, but let us search and know what the word is to us, then act faithfully. Another lesson seen in this narrative is that the Lord always beholds the sins of men and reproves them, and if they do not forsake them He will judge them with equity and justice. He had informed the king that a wicked course, such as he had pursued, would lead to utter destruction, and we see the literal fulfillment of all the Lord said He would inflict on both the king and the altar, and the name of the man given that should perform it, though he was not born, and so it all occurred and, as these are types, their antitypes must follow.

First Kings xvi:29, Ahab comes to the throne of

Israel; his reign was wicked and notable for his idolatrous connection with Baal worship. His wife, Jezebel, with him, bring to the world lessons of importance, for when they had lived in the ways of sin and of their fallen and depraved hearts, until the righteous judgments of the Lord fell on them, they were like the people of to-day under similar circumstances, and did not look at home for the cause, but charged it on the prophet of the Lord, which was to charge it on the Lord. They had forsaken the Lord and given themselves to the service of Baal, the most popular of idols, and they led Israel from the Lord to Baal and would seek the life of one that would reprove them and tell them the truth as Elijah did. It is plain that the Bible represents all idolatry as Spiritual adultery, the most corrupting, degrading, defiling evil that ever did, or ever can, enter into human society. But these idolatries were types that pointed to the Christian or gospel day and age of the world, and they have their anti-types of the present time, and in this very highly favored land of the United States of America. Idolatry is Spiritual adultery to-day as really as it was then, and there is likely more of it, and it is practiced under more aggravated circumstances, and with vastly greater light. The true definition of idolatry is to seek for, or strive for, or to accept anything as an object of trust, or to in any way rely on anything other than the Almighty. For the Lord is the bridegroom, and His people are His bride, namely His church, and for any people to seek or accept another source of trust than the Lord, is like the wife that seeks and accepts her luxuries, or comforts, or pleasures from another man than her husband. It is infidelity. Among the various forms of idolatry to-day may be mentioned free masonry, which claims to be the oldest, and with it all like organizations that meet in secret counsel for mutual protection or support in times of emergency, and all such as remove the trust from the living God. All this is literal idolatry, and Spiritual adultery, as well as insurance of life or property, lightning rods and the like.

But of the objects of ungodly alliance, the chief may be seen in the medical profession. There are but few persons in the world that have an idea of the amount of human life that falls a needless sacrifice every year to what is called the medical science.

It is quoted from Dr. Rush's work in these words: "Dissection daily convince us of our ignorance of the seat of disease, and cause us to blush at our prescriptions." A practioner of more than ordinary reliance both for truth and skill, said that in a given time, in the town wherein he practiced, there had been about one thousand interments, and as many as one-half of the subjects ought to have regained their health. Very many writings and expressions tell us that quite a large proportion of the deaths that occur in civilization is caused by the medical profession, though the public will not believe testimony against that profession, though themselves be the witnesses. Surely Baal was a fit type of them. But men must die. But a more burning shame for civilization is that when our friends are dead, and we give them a respectable burial, the grave is robbed of its sacred trust; the body is gone! Not only so but cases are not wanting published by the press, in which persons have been murdered expressly for dissection, and it has been published that some very popular institutions have had their dissection tables furnished with subjects that had been murdered for their use expressly.

One young man recovering from fever was induced into a thick woods. A strong man bound his body, round arms and hands with a strong sash made for the purpose, then covered the face with a plaster made for the purpose of hastening death and preventing alarm, but he uttered one shriek in the scuffle; two men heard it and reached him in time to save him. It was found that the man was hired by an institution not far away. Search was made, and there was found evidence that various ones who had been missed years before had ended their days there, and proof was found that for a number of years had murdered subjects for dissection. This was published in a church paper several years ago, the particulars having been forgotten.

A case was published in Cincinnati, about the year 1884, of a principal telling his resurrectionist that he must have a subject this week if he, the resurrectionist, had to tap somebody on the head, (testimony so published.) The resurrectionist was a colored man, who took whisky to a house where three colored people lived, an old man and his wife and niece, and gave them of the whisky till opportunity offered, and then tapped the three on the head so quickly there was no time for alarm. He cleaned up the place and took the bodies to the place appointed, and received $30 each for those bodies. The resurrectionist was put on trial, but no account taken of the man that hired him to do the murder. The Baal cruelty was terrible, but when a habit of that character is spread over civilization, Baal only could make a type of it.

But the destruction of human life by medicine and the robbing of the graves of the same bodies that died under the influence of their treatment, both fall very short of being the greatest objection to that antitype of Baal idolatry. But the man obstetrician may well be considered so.

In solution of Bible problems, there is an expression on that subject that is offensive to some, but herein consider the Word, on the subject. When the serpent tempted the woman to eat of the forbidden tree, she answered that God hath said we shall not. But how often must we find that God hath said any one thing to make it valid to us? Will one time establish the thing that is said? In Proverbs Chapter vi:27 it says:

Can a man take fire in his bosom and his clothes not be burned?

28th. Can one go on hot coals and his feet not be burned?

29th. So he that goeth into his neighbor's wife: whosoever toucheth her shall not be innocent.

In 27th and 28th verses the strongest figure in nature is brought with which to compare the topic under consideration. The first clause of the 29th does not convey sense only to define the topic to be adultery, but it does that unmistakably.

The second clause of the 29th verse defines what adultery is more in particular. Now it is impossible to see a less meaning in these brief expressions, than the going in to his neighbor's wife in the first clause and the "whosoever toucheth her" in the second clause of the 29th verse, makes the two acts equally guilty, and means the same thing, and both alike are adultery, and that is forbidden in the seventh commandment.

In 1 Timothy ii:15, there is a promise to woman at such a crisis on certain conditions, but it is not if she have the doctor. Is that promise to be relied on?

But the passage quoted in Proverbs clearly shows that what God hath said makes the man official at child-birth a species of adultery. Exodus xx:14, is the seventh commandment in which God hath said, "Thou shalt not commit adultery." How will that compare with Baal.

Now, let all the earth say what they choose concerning the propriety or impropriety of men practicing obstetrics. Here is one, "God hath said they shall not," and he has shown us that it is adultery, and that is the blackest crime that man can commit against man except murder. Also the Bible shows clearly that woman practiced these things when the Lord ruled his people, and it is said by one writer on the subject that it was never known among Christians until the crown of France introduced it for purposes of concealment, probably in the fifteenth century. But it was practiced among the heathen likely in the days of Solomon, and the passage herein considered was to forewarn Christians that the practice would as surely burn the spirit of Christ out of their heart, as fire would burn the clothing or the feet, if it come in contact with them. And not only so but read French and English authors, Robert Gooch and others, on female complaints and note their counsel to the young physician how to treat the female that comes to his room for advice, or treatment, that if the case will admit of such idea, call it sexual derangement and propose an internal scrutiny, and says, "Some may object, but press it, press it, if they do not need it, you do need it in your experience and in your practice." So that this boasted science of medicine claims the mastery over every species of female chastity and delicacy or modesty.

Shall not a just God be avenged on such corrupt nations as these? But if this planet was not ordained for the absolutely necessary design to develope the fruit of wrong in all forms and magnitudes, then how would it be possible to account for the existence of these monstrous things? Consider how wide spread these monstrous habits are, and how could society be less than a mass of corruption?

Verily the type that Baal made was terrible, but the antitype is incalculably more so. These Bible types are messages to the church and to the world today, and they should not be trifled with. We can not afford it. It was our God that prepared them. It was our God that sent them to us. It is our God that will require them at our hand. Let the Ahabs and Jezebels of all the church be warned if they will, but if they will not God is not mocked.

But O man or woman that wishes to be governed by what God hath said, come out from among them. You will have to oppose church and state, your own preacher, and likely nearly all the members of society you have hitherto lived in, but fly, fly, fly like Lot did from Sodom.

You may think that I might well fear to take such ground against all the civilized world, and so I have feared the last fifty years nearly, but now I see that what God hath said in the record that he has left us, so clearly binds his words to that meaning and can not admit of any other, that it seems not only admissible, but duty clearly requires it of me. And though these practices are so nearly universal with a very few conscientious exceptions, yet that is no reason that we should not accept what God hath said, "Ye shall not." Let God be true, but every man a liar. But Baal, the type, seemed to the prophet Elijah to be even more universal, for he answered the Lord that he only was left in Israel, and they sought his life to take it away.

Now tell us all you divines in the orthodox world, is there or is there not wisdom in these scriptures, and if revelation could be perfect without these passages? If Baal was not a type then it is the greatest batch of nonsense that the whole human race finds to read, but if it was a type, it was needful that it should show its antitype with perfect clearness, and that the antitype would be something vast in its nature, but nevertheless it was necessary to suffer such a state of things to exist, that every form and degree of depravity and sin and wrong in its blackest and deepest colors should be developed, and put on endless exhibition, and at the same time make revelation that will eternally show the throne to be guiltless. But the entire amount of evil is the work of the universal enemy, the mischevious and vast power of wrong.

The distinguishable difference is seen in the end to which these two remarkable men came, both the king and the prophet. The king with the kingdom at his command sought the life of Elijah, for the king had put Naboth to death for his vineyard, and the dogs had licked the blood of Naboth. The prophet had met and reproved the king, and said to him, "In the place where dogs licked the blood of Naboth, shall dogs lick thy blood, even thine," and not long afterward the blood of this self same king Ahab was licked up by the dogs in the very spot where the the dogs had licked the blood of Naboth.

But what comes of the prophet that stood single handed and alone against the king and his corrupt kingdom? We see him and Elisha going together, and coming to the Jordan, and the waters part and they walk over unmolested. They walk on a little farther and the Lord sends a chariot and horses of fire, and takes the prophet without his tasting death. Verily, verily, it is profitable to serve the Lord.

If I did not think that I had proven and established the philosophical relation of all that class of passages

I would give it some attention here, but I think it not necessary.

But how is this God-forbidden and God-dishonoring practice to be overcome, seeing it is so near universal that no sufficient number is left to overcome it? If one household raise a family that keep themselves pure from those habits that the Word forbids, that household does overcome for so much of the world as stands in opposition to it, if that is a whole county, or a whole State, or the country entire, if there are none to stand with it. But the heathen world that does not practice such things will be witnesses for the Lord that this promise is not a failure to them, but was ever true to them when conditions were met by the creature.

Hence there are living witnesses in every age to indemnify the Lord beside the word of revelation that is given to the world.

And this Word that says, "Thou shalt not," even that word will stand exonerated at the judgment in every particular.

2 Kings ii:23-27. When Elisha was mocked by the children he cursed them in the name of the Lord, and two bears tore, and we suppose killed, forty-two of them. The Lord brought all this about, to show by its type the guilt both of the children who were made an example of and suffered, and also of the parents who suffered their children to pour their con-

tempt on either the cause, or the people of the Lord, to any great extent.

2 Kings v:1-27. It is not hard to understand the type that Naaman's leprosy makes. Naaman in the type is the unrenewed heart, and the leprosy is the sin of heart and life. The prophet was one who spoke and did just what the Lord gave him to speak and to do, and he represented the Lord. When Naaman felt the need of healing and heard of the Lord's power to heal, he went to seek the Lord to be healed. That is the sinner who is convicted and seeking pardon from the Lord. The prophet sent a man to instruct him what to do. And the Lord sends the minister to instruct the spiritual leper. When he was offended it represents the pride and wisdom of this world that thinks the gospel is too common, too simple, too low for them, and they are offended. When he was admonished by his servant that it was easy to do, and he decided to try, it represents those who humble themselves and accept the gospel. The cleansing the leprosy is the best type of conversion that nature affords. Naaman wishes to reward the prophet, but the prophet disdained to take money or reward. So does every servant of the cross disdain to take reward for instructing others in the way of life.

The servant of the prophet goes after Naaman and takes a reward from him, and when he returned he did not tell the prophet what he had done; but the prophet told him, and reproved him and said the leprosy of Naaman should cleave to him and his seed forever, and he went out a leper white as snow.

Here the servant typified anyone living among Christians, and professing to be a Christian, but who covets, and obtains money or goods in some way that is not clearly right, and tries to cover it up with false pretense. Whether it is a true Christian, or a pretender only that does the like, the spiritual leprosy will cleave to him. The narrative is full of valuable lessons.

In the sixth chapter is revealed the Lord's care over His servant. When Syria warred against Israel, the Syrian king learned that the prophet Elisha would tell the king of Israel all the Syrians' plans, and the king of Syria sent horses and chariots and a great host to take Elisha and his servant. In the morning the servant saw the great host that had come to take the two men, the prophet and his servant, and he was alarmed. But Elisha said, "Lord, I pray thee open his eyes that he may see," and the servant saw the mountain full of horses and chariots of fire round about Elisha. And when they had come down to him, Elisha prayed to the Lord to smite the people with blindness. How short were these two prayers of the prophet! But how promptly they were answered; the one for the servant to see, and the other for the people to be made blind. Here the man they were sent to arrest said to them, "Follow me and I will bring you to the man whom ye seek." They followed him blindly but willingly into their enemies' capital, where, if they had been treated as they would have treated their enemies, they would have been hopeless as well as helpless.

Elisha prayed that they might see, and they saw themselves in the midst of Samaria. This type is a promise of the Lord to all that separate themselves from the world, and serve the Lord in spirit and in truth, for the world will be arrayed against them to a greater or less extent. But let all such observe a few things, as do not say or do anything that is wrong, be reserved, let the Lord rule the whole matter, and victory to them is certain. These promises are given in words, but words may be wrongly interpreted or misunderstood, but the type cannot. When the Syrians came to Samaria, Elisha would not smite them, but bade the Samaratans to give them food and drink, that they might be refreshed and go home to their masters.

Now, herein was the wisdom and power of the Lord revealed to the heathens of Syria, that the weapons of the spiritual warfare are not carnal but mighty, for when Israel had the Syrians in their power, the prophet had great provisions made for them, and when they had eaten and drank, he sent them away and they went to their masters. So the bands of Syria came no more into the land of Israel. But if they had smitten them with sword and bow, they would have been back with regular army to take vengeance on them. But when the prophet treated them with good for evil, it had a power over them that sword and bow could not have. The type is of great value, and proves that the spiritual weapons of warfare are stronger than carnal weapons, when viewed in a physical light.

But Syria must make another type of great value, and it was by the king of Syria gathering all his host and going up and beseiging Samaria until the famine was so great that women were so pressed with hunger that they cooked and ate their own infant children. When the king knew such to be the case he sent messengers to put the prophet Elisha to death because he had not obtained relief of the Lord, but soon went and revoked the order. Then the prophet told them there should be plenty by this time to-morrow, but one of them doubted the word. The prophet told the one that doubted that he should see it, but should not eat of it.

There were four lepers shut out of the city and they came to the Syrian camp to beg food, but found the army had fled in great alarm and left their provisions. The Lord had caused them to hear a great noise, like the approach of a great army, and the Syrians, supposing there was another army hired to come against them, retreated in haste, leaving everything behind them. The four lepers told their brethren in the city, and at the hour the prophet had said that food should be sold so low in the gates of Samaria, so it was done. But the man who had doubted the word of the Lord, by the prophet, was put in charge of the gate of Samaria, and when he had seen the food sold the people trampled on him and he died. By this type we are taught that the Lord rules the wars of the earth, did then and does yet, and always will. He also rules the destiny of nations as well as individuals. In these types there is the clearest revelation that the Lord has the most absolute control over all nature, and that it is as easy to control anything out of its common order as it is to control the same things in their natural order. All nature belongs to the Lord, and is as perfectly at His command as the hand of a man is at the man's command; and there is no exception in nature, neither earth, nor air, nor sea, nor beast, nor fish, nor fowl, nor insect, nor creeping thing. When these things are all seen and clearly understood, the servant of the Lord can trust him perfectly until the last moment, and when they are realized, it is impossible to trust anything else.

In the seventeenth chapter there is a type of that part of the visible church of Christ that professes to be the disciples of Christ, but does not possess, nor try to possess the spirit of Christ. From the event of Israel becoming a separate people from Judah, and assuming another government they seemed to sin almost continually. Only when the Lord would give them over to an enemy that would oppress them, they would cry to the Lord and He would raise up deliverance for them. These are true types of the great army of Christians that do not exact of themselves a holy life, but take an erroneous course, at first very little, and that little leads to more until they delight in something sinful, until the day of trouble comes, or grief, or want. Then they think on the Lord, and call upon Him and He relieves them, but only to repeat the same thing over and over. And the oftener it is repeated the more hardened they become, until forbearance ceases to be a virtue, like it did with Israel, and the Lord does with them as He did with Israel, for He cast Israel out of His sight, so it is written. For Assyrians, a much mightier people than was Syria, that warred with them before, carried Israel away captive into their far-off land from which they were never suffered to return, but dwelt with heathens until they themselves became heathens. So must it be spiritually with such as live in the church, but do not live in Christ nor have Christ live in them. When the Lord cast off Israel He restrained the tribe of Judah for very much further usefulness; but when Israel went into hopeless exile it was but just to them, but was overruled to make the plainest possible type of the millions that profess Christ and wear the highly exalted name of Christian, but do not possess nor desire to possess His nature. Millions to-day may see in that type the relation they sustain to the latter, and if they do not move from the ground they now occupy they will be driven into hopeless exile, spiritually. But Judah was the type of the Lord's favored people, and was known to be so, for when Senacherib, king of Assyria, invaded Judah, also supposing it to be a small thing to take Jerusalem and make a clean sweep of the entire people and made his lofty threatenings, the Lord heard them and said, "I will defend this city to save it for My own sake, and My servant David's sake. And it came to pass that night that the angel of the Lord went out and smote in the camp of the Assyrians an hundred and four score and five thousand. And when they arose early in the morning behold they were dead corpses." Now was not the city of Jerusalem defended most signally? But why could it not be done for the sake of Jerusalem and the Jews, for it was done for the Lord's sake and for His servant David's sake? Because Jerusalem and the Jews were too wicked to be worthy of such favors, and it was needful to make it known that it was not done for their sakes, but for the Lord's sake. Then why suffer the whole transaction at all? Because that very narrative was needful for a type of the Lord's power and care over Christ's true people, of whom the Jews were a type, and it was also needful to make a revelation that is not made anywhere else, and revelation must be perfect. But they were saved for the Lord's sake, and the Lord was identical with the Son of David who was promised, and who was the root as well as the offspring of David. The Jews and their city were required much longer to perfect that revelation that the Son of David designed to make perfect by them. All philosophically reasonable, and the Bible could not have been perfect without this very narrative. It was soon made manifest that it was not for the sake of the Jews, nor their city, that the Lord defended them against the Assyrians, for the wickedness of the Jews soon became so great that they, like Israel, were carried away into captivity though not hopeless like Israel. In this carrying away into Babylon is a type of backsliding from a sanctified life. For certainly Judah was the type of the perfect Christian, and their land was the type of the kingdom of Christ in the Christian heart. When the narrative of their captivity is read of their servitude, the scornful relation they were held in, how they were despised and set at naught, and taunted, it is seen to be the clearest type of the horrors of the life of the backslider. When the enemy carried away to heathen Babylon all the precious things of the temple, and all the people of importance and burned the house of the Lord with fire, and burned all the valuable houses, and broke down the wall of Jerusalem round about, so that all seemed like desolation, it represents the despair that reigns in the backslidden heart. When the holy and beautiful house in which their fathers worshipped was burned with fire, and all their pleasant things laid waste, the type is perfect of the backslider.

But though the Lord drove his people into bondage or captivity into a heathen land (that was a true type of the backslidden heart, the most desolate relation that any one can sustain), yet the Lord was most signally with them there, and revealed Himself to that heathen nation by them. He also distinguished His people in a very notable manner, as in case of Esther and Mordecai, when Haman took measures to have all the Jews put to death, and the day was appointed for the execution of that work, and Haman had made a gallows fifty cubits high on which to hang Mordecai. He came into the court to speak to the king to hang Mordecai, but the Lord had brought all things in readiness to send Haman to do Mordecai honor. A few minutes later, and the queen tells the king that she and her people are decreed to become the victims of Haman's malice, and as the king's anger kindles at Haman, one tells him of the gallows that Haman had prepared for Mordecai. Then the king gave orders to hang Haman thereon. How remarkable that from the time Haman came into the court to request the king to hang Mordecai on the gallows Haman had prepared for him, that Haman himself had not time to be at rest until he was a lifeless lump of clay hanging on the gallows whereon he had designed to hang Mordecai! Verily, verily, O, man, it is safe to trust in the Lord, though all may seem dark even to the last moment! How valuable to the people of the earth are the types and lessons brought to view by the Babylonian captivity! What revelations are therein made of the Lord to that heathen people, and also to all the world, as well as to the church! Nebuchadnezzar's dream (recorded in 2d chapter of Daniel). He forgets his own dream, and he would put his wise men to death if they did not tell him his dream and the interpretation. The Lord was bringing all this about for the purpose of making a revelation of Himself to that heathen people, as well as all people to whom revelation would come; everything is so wisely ordered that his condescension and favor to man were as valuable and praiseworthy as if there had been no other object in view but the benefit of the human race, and yet that was the smallest part of the design of revelation. But Daniel, this disdained captive, in the strength of his Lord steps into the presence of the monarch with astonishing boldness and says, "We will tell the king his dream." Likely no one believed he could, until he spoke with such assurance and told the dream that the dreamer himself had forgotten. This was no doubt the most wonderful talk that ever fell on the ears of that monarch, and it prepared him to believe the interpretation which Daniel, the captive, told him. But what a change of affairs was displayed the next moment, for that monarch of the world that would have disdained to suffer the captive Jew to come into his presence in times when there were no disturbing influences around him, now falls upon his face and worships Daniel, and commands that they should offer an oblation (Dan. ii:46) and sweet odors to him, and acknowledge Daniel's God to be the true God. After all this, the king made the golden image, but the Lord's people would not worship it, and the penalty was that they be put into the furnace, the heat of which was so terrible that to look into it was like looking into the sun. But when it came to the test they chose to be put into the furnace, rather than to bow or fall down and worship the king's idol. When they were put into the furnace the heat was so great that it slew the men who took them up. But the three that were cast into the fire met the form of a fourth, that was like the Son of God, and the fire did not hurt them. Then was Nebuchadnezzar, the king, astonished, and said "Did not we cast three men bound into the midst of the fire?" and they said, "True, O king." And he said " Lo, I see four men, loose, walking in the midst of the fire, and they have no hurt, and the form of the fourth is like the Son of God." But mark how the king was changed toward these men, for he said to them, " Ye servants of the most high God come forth and come hither." And when they came out there was not a hair of their heads singed, nor the smell of fire about them, nor were their clothes changed. What a type that is, that has cheered the hearts of millions of men and women since that vast exhibition of divine power which was then, and is ever round and about the true servant of God! And this very type is the strongest promise that it is, or could be possible to make to the human race, that whosoever will choose the Lord for the object of their services and fidelity that when the enemy surrounds them with trouble and danger and threatens death in its most frightful form, let them be assured that the Lord is there; let them be firm and faithful as the Hebrews were, and the Lord will bring the best possible results out of it, which will abide everlastingly. But besides all this, including the millions that literally perish in the fires of persecution, there are other millions that have been in the furnace of affliction, or tribulation, and this very narrative has strengthened them and carried them through with the brightest victory. The form of the fourth is always there. No less profitable to the Christian is the narrative as a type, of Daniel when he was cast into the den of lions. The government officials envied Daniel because he was wiser and stood higher in the king's favor than they. But how should they get him removed out of their way? They saw the unswerving fidelity of Daniel to his God, and they might by that means succeed. So they obtained a decree that no one should ask any petition of any one for thirty days, except from the king only, and that those who should must be cast into the den of lions. But when Daniel knew the writing was signed he opened his window toward Jerusalem, and kneeled upon his knees and prayed, and gave thanks before his God as he did aforetime. Then they brought the matter before the king and claimed the decree, and Daniel was cast into the den of lions. But Daniel's God was there, and the lions were innocent as kittens. Did not the Lord and Daniel have a pleasant night together among the lions? But the king could not sleep, and at the dawn of day he was at the den and called Daniel with an interest, and also a suspense that was unknown to him before. But Daniel answered, and the king commanded, and Daniel was taken out of the den safe and sound. Then the king commanded to bring his accusers and to cast them into the same den, and their wives and their children. But the lions broke their bones before they reached the bottom of the den. How very plainly this type points to these very days and years of the nineteenth century! For when the Son of David was on trial before the governor who was judge, he (the governor) said, "Take ye him and crucify him, for I find no fault in him." Millions of others since that have been the objects of the malice of the wicked because they could find no fault in them, and they want to cast them into the furnace, or the den of lions, or crucify them. And when the law does not permit these modes of taking vengeance, they crucify them in their reputation, or their usefulness, or in their property, and often assassinate them. Any way at all, but get them out of the way when we can find no fault in them.

These last two narratives are recorded in the book of Daniel, but were transacted in heathen Babylon, when Israel were captives in that heathen land, and although they well merited the terrible judgment to be driven into captivity, yet it was so wisely overruled that the page of their history while they were in Babylon, was as conspicuous as any other part of their history. The types are eminently useful to the Christian church, showing the dreadful relation and condition of the backslider, as well as how sin was met and conquered, as in case of Haman and Mordicai. These types show Christians just how to meet and conquer sin.

First and second Chronicles: The most important passages in them were noticed in first and second Kings, and as the object of this brief writing is to compare the scripture with the introductory chapters, so far as is needful to show clear reason and harmony in all the Bible, pass Chronicles, and consider the book of Ezra.

The people of Israel have been noticed as the type of the world in sin, of the conviction of the penitent, of the new heart, or conversion to Christ, and the Christian led through difficulties, and of the Christian searching the scriptures (the law from Sinai). Christians see in the scriptures the promise of the perfect heart and life, in which Christ would reign (Canaan). But they fear, and turn their course into the wilderness, and cross the Jordan into the promised land, and become a type of cleansing the heart, and of the Christian's inheritance. But for their unfaithfulness, backsliding, they were driven into captivity (Babylon). But now we come to Ezra. Now is the book of Ezra the type of a revival of pure and true Godliness in the Christian church, and the building up of the Spiritual house of the Lord? If this is the sense in which we should understand Ezra, and the design for which the book of Ezra was written, it will be well to notice narrowly what lessons the type teaches us.

The first thing to notice is that the Lord called Cyrus king of Persia both into power, and also to use his power to move Irael into action, and the call or appointment was predicted before Cyrus was born. But he came into power and issued his proclamation to Israel to go and build the house of the Lord at Jerusalem, and delivered to the Jews all the vessels of the temple to carry back to Jerusalem. So the Lord moves every true revival of his cause in the world in all ages of Christendom. But many of them went and set everything in order, and gave money for the expenses. (That was the road to a true revival then, and is yet.) Then they built an altar and presented their offering to the Lord (the people offering themselves) and they established the regular sacrificial service of the Lord. When they had the foundation laid they set all things in their place and worshipped before the Lord, and there was a loud shout and much rejoicing. So it is with Christians when the Lord's work moves favorably. Now, when their adversaries heard that they were building the temple they came to Zerubbabel and to the chief of the fathers, and said unto them, "Let us build with you, for we seek your God as ye do, and we do sacrifice unto Him." But Zerubbabel and Joshua and the rest of the fathers of Israel said unto them, "Ye have nothing to do with us to build a house unto the Lord our God, but we ourselves will build unto the Lord God of Israel, as king Cyrus, the king of Persia, hath commanded us." But soon as they were refused by the builders they showed more plainly who they were, for they were enemies with all their ability to be so. They hindered them by all means in their power, and wrote to the king, the successor of Cyrus, until they obtained a decree to cause the work to cease. Now here is the opposition that the true work of the Lord meets when true Christians are favored with a revival. The work stopped for a time, but the Lord raised up two prophets, Haggai and Zachariah, and encouraged the work.

The work was resumed and so was the opposition. Their enemies used all means in their power to hinder the work, but they could not until the matter came before the king. But when the next decree came the command was to let them build the house of the Lord, and furnish them money and food and beasts for sacrifices, and that these should be given them daily, and that whosoever should alter this word let timber be pulled down from his house and being set up let him be hanged thereon. Here is a guarantee to the man of the cross that is engaged in a revival and is sure that himself walks with the Lord, let the opposition take what course it may, let him be confident that the Lord will make the effort serve the best purpose that it can serve, whether there is a visible revival or not. This very narrative of Ezra is for the express purpose of showing that the truly called and sent servant of the cross will have enemies anywhere only among the cross bearing Christians. Then these enemies were forced to become helpers in the work of the Lord which they had tried so hard to destroy. So it often occurs that the strongest enemies to a revival become converted, and wheel into line and are profitable helps in the work. One very important feature of this type that is seen in Ezra is that when the Lord sends his servants to build up his spiritual house in the form of a revival, that any person, whether high or low, either in the church or in the world, who would introduce and recommend doctrines or practices lower than the Bible standard of purity, piety and godliness should be promptly rejected, and any church organization whose principles are lower than the Bible should also be promptly rejected. Purity is worth more than numbers, and to trust in the Lord for strength and for success is better than the strength of the world, only keep the offering pure. Ezra would not be complete if that part had been omitted, and the temple could not have been built if they had joined with the heathen to build it, for it was not the property of men, and its design was the type of spiritual purity.

In chapter seven Ezra and others of Judah are

commissioned to go to Jerusalem from Babylon and carry a great amount of wealth which was to be used on and about the temple. The journey was long, requiring nearly four months. The road was full of danger for the enemy mentioned in the narrative was likely to attack them, as were also robbers, pirates and various other companies of men seeking plunder of whomsoever they met. But Ezra proclaimed a fast to seek the favor of the Lord, for he said he was ashamed to require a band of soldiers and horsemen to help them against the enemy in the way, because he had professed to the king to trust in the Lord. "So we fasted and besought our God for this, and he was entreated of us."

Now what was all this written here for? Professing Christian tell us, if it was not to show that the Lord alone should or could be trusted by his true followers. Then where is the foundation on which you build your hope, if you enter the lodge of any secret order for the hope of reliance on them?

I once heard in a lecture of a Free Masonry that a man at sea with the ships crew was taken by pirates and the crew murdered, but he gave the masonic sign of distress and found a brother among the pirates that saved him. Three other narratives were related of the same character, one among land pirates, but in all four of the narratives the company were all murdered but one, and that one was saved only by finding a brother Free Mason among the murderers to whom they were oath bound in a brotherhood that was stronger than the bond that binds murderers and pirates together. And still there are Free Masons who profess to be bound in a brotherhood to the Lord Jesus Christ! Shame, shame, O shame!

One more narrative in Ezra: that is concerning the people of Israel who had married strange wives or heathen women. In all places where such wickedness is written in the Bible it is the type of any one professing to live the Christian life, but holding fast to something else as a reliance but the Lord. The spirit of Christ demands that Christians shall rely on Christ alone, and that it is their voluntary choice. All other sources of reliance must like the strange wives, be put away, for they were all put away with all their children. Not only so but when the proclamation was made for all to attend to this business those who did not come up within the three days prescribed, forfeited their substance and were separated from their people. Is this type worth the notice of smart men, wise and learned? Or may not the heathen, which is the infidel now, say to the Christian world, "Where is your God?" A little comment on Ezra and Nehemiah and their important uses or the objects they were designed to accomplish.

To make the real design plain in all its bearings is likely as difficult a task as any part of the Bible, for if nothing can be seen in them, but the record or history they furnish, they only seem like other histories of governments that have only men for their authors and would be unworthy of a place in a revelation made by infinite wisdom, designed for endless usefulness.

If they enter into the legislative records of a political power, then they are entitled to full credit by all political powers on earth. But if they are a type of reviving the interest of the salvation of the entire human race, and as plain as if the type was the only object for which they were made, then that is a second item embraced in these narratives that is worth all they cost, and fully worthy of their author. But if, at the same time, the same writing is a complete type of the revival of the pure, true doctrines of the Bible, in the church and in the world, (for in the type the walls were the protection of Zion, and in the antitype the pure, true doctrines of the Bible are the protection of the Christian church,) then that is a third item worth the whole cost of the whole transaction, and worthy of its author. A fourth item is that they make a revelation of the Lord on the subject of revivals which is not made elsewhere and each one different from the other.

But a fifth item of importance in Ezra and Nehemiah is that they are the clearest type of certain sins of the Christian dispensation, as how sinners will stoop in their wickedness in trying to defeat a revival of the Lord's cause in the world.

Sometimes when the true messengers of the Lord will raise the standard of the cross where the Lord puts it, and hold the written word up to its high and holy eminence, the messengers of Satan will come and propose to join them in the revival. But they only seek its corruption and ruin, or sometimes they try to pour their disdain on the work to destroy it, like as when the wall was to be built. All of these very different items and others, are each one made as plain as if the sole object had been for the sake of only one of these. And still some doubt who their author might have been, and some in high places in church are hunting over ancient and modern literature to find the names of those who wrote the several parts of the Bible, in order to establish their authorship. Is it any wonder that there are infidels in the world?

Ezra has been considered a type of revival in the Christian church, not of doctrines, but the increase of numbers and powers of the church. But Nehemiah is the type of reviving the doctrines of the scriptures; for the walls were to Zion, or Jerusalem, the same as the true doctrine of the scriptures are to the Christian church. In either case these were the defenses.

Now, when Nehemiah knew the distressed condition of Jerusalem, he wept and mourned certain days, and fasted, and then besought the Lord by prayer and confessions of sins of Judah; beseaching the Lord for Jerusalem and the Jews. After the fasting and prayer, the king gave Nehemiah permission to go to Jerusalem with an escort, and also the privilege of timber to make the gates that the work might be commenced. But so soon as the work started, the heathen enemies of the Lord were devising every possible means to stop the progress of the work, for they taunted them and tried to deceive and alarm them. So it was when the reformers, Luther, Calvin, and the Wesleys and others, commenced to build up new systems of doctrine, or really to rebuild the old system that, like the walls had been broken down, and it is the same way yet. If the most corrupt pretentions are reproved, the enemies of the truth will break the reformers down if possible, but the Lord has left them instructions in the books of Ezra and Nehemiah.

Nehemiah breathed forth the most devout and earnest prayer, and so do the Christians. The heathen conspired to come and fight them, and stop the work. Our laws forbid that in its literal form, but they will come and want to debate, or get up a dispute, or anything to succeed in causing the work to cease. But they of old made their prayer to their

God, and set a watch against them day and night, and this is the course of the Christian.

Nehemiah inspired the people with boldness, saying, "Be not afraid of them," and so does the Christian leader encourage the people to fight, not with carnal weapons, but those that are mighty through God to the pulling down of strongholds. After that, half of the men held weapons of defense, while the other half wrought in the work. "They which builded on the wall, and they that bare burdens, with those that laded, everyone with one of his hands wrought in the work, and with the other hand held a weapon. For the builders everyone had his sword girded by his side, and so builded, and he that sounded the trumpet was by me. And so they labored and held weapons from the rising of the morning till the stars appeared. And they lodged in Jerusalem for purpose of defense, and none of them put off their clothes except for washing."

Now, in these last remarks we see the estimate that the Lord puts on the establishing and maintaining the pure and true doctrines of his word. The carnal weapons and the vigilance seen in the narrative are the true type of the spiritual contention for the pure theology in the Christian church, for to be acceptable the doctrines must be pure.

In the fifth chapter, the poor in the land said they had come into distress because other men had their land, and their children were in bondage, and they could not redeem them.

Now here is one of the best lessons that can be found anywhere. Nehemiah told those men that had taken for pledge the land of their poor brother, that after the ability of himself and those that were with him, they had redeemed their brethren, the Jews which were sold to the heathen, and said, "Will ye even sell your brethren?" But when he set up his own course of action, and the nobles knew it, they could not answer him. They restored to every one his inheritance. The example of Nehemiah was a controlling power over the people.

And now, O Christian man or woman, if the Lord has committed to your trust or to my trust, either time, or money, or property, or influence, what higher use can we make of it than to induce others to works of righteousness? But when their enemies heard that the wall was built all but setting up the doors, they sent unto Nehemiah four times to meet them in some village, that they might do him mischief. But he answered them that he was doing a great work— "why should the work cease?" What an unanswerable question when one is doing the Lord's work with success.

But after all this the enemy sent again to Nehemiah, saying that he and the Jews were preparing to rebel, and that it should be reported to the king. But Nehemiah replied to the message that no such things were done as he said, "but thou feignest them out of thine own heart," and again he utters his remarkable prayer to his God for help. After all this they said to him, "Let us shut ourselves up in the temple," lest their enemies should come at night and kill Nehemiah. But he asked in reply if such a man as he was should flee, or go into the temple to save his life? "I will not go in." But he that said it was hired by the enemy that they might make Nehemiah afraid and sin in the act of obeying them. But again Nehemiah flies to his stronghold in fervent prayer to his God for help and defense. It is noteworthy that the last item on record before the wall was finished was that Tobiah and Sanballat hired that false prophet to put Nehemiah in fear, that the work at the last might be a failure, the most perfect type of the way that the world and the worldly element in church bring their force against any upbuilding of the cause even in the days of gospel light. But the type goes on and shows more of the opposition the servants of the cross may expect when they are engaged in a revival of either doctrine or practice of Bible purity.

Not unfrequently the opposition is found in high places in church, for Tobiah and Sanballat were the leading men in all the opposition to Nehemiah and to the work that his Lord had sent him to accomplish.

Nevertheless there were leading men of the Jews who should have been faithful to the Lord and His servant Nehemiah, that were allied to Tobiah, and conspired with him against Nehemiah and against his work. But after all this incessant opposition to the Lord's work these conspirators furnish another type of the difficulty that the true servant and people of the Lord, and truly called and sent ministers of the cross have to contend with in the nineteenth century. In chapter thirteen we read that Elishia, the priest, having charge or oversight of the chamber of the house of our God, was allied to Tobiah. "And he had prepared for him a great chamber, where aforetime they laid the meat offerings, the frankincense, and the vessels, and the tithes of the corn, the new wine and the oil, which was commanded to be given to the Levites, and the singers, and the porters, and the offerings of the priests." Here we see that when this Tobiah could not prevent the true doctrines of the Word from being established (or the wall built), that he effected an alliance with the priest, the man having authority. So the openly professed enemy of the Lord aspires to a high place in the Lord's church by his alliance with its lawfully installed ministers and with all his corrupt life, and bold opposition to the Lord's servants and their righteous work, he is installed in the temple and makes carnal use of that part that was sanctified to the sacred purpose of storing of the support of the Levites, and the singers, and the porters, and the offerings of the priests. These were put out, and heathen man with his heathen customs was put in possession. Is not this re-enacted when the worldly minister is installed in any church, and introduces the festival, the supper, the feast, the play, or any other entertainment, but the solemn worship of his Lord?

Now when the Lord's true minister of the cross meets opposition to the true doctrines, and must fight through on every inch of the road, but finally, by clear immovable argument establishes the whole Bible in the light of the strongest reason, then the Sanballats and Tobiahs will step forth and say "Well, I always knew that. I always believed and held that the only correct doctrine and they assume to have been the main element in bringing out their doctrines, but really they were the Tobiahs to corrupt them." When Nehemiah came to Jerusalem and learned what was done, he cast out all the household stuff out of the chamber and commanded the chamber to be cleansed, and brought again the things that belonged there.

Now can there be found in this whole earth, outside of the Bible, any two interests so far apart in point of time and circumstances so different, that the one will so minutely represent the other, as Nehemiah represents the Christian church to-day, and the establishing of the pure doctrines of the Bible? And still there are those in high relation that are hunting testimony to the authorship of parts of the Bible. The Sanballets and the Tobiahs never can find it.

The book of Esther has been considered in connection with the captivity into Babylon.

The next department to consider is Job, and as the object of these pages is to prove that the Bible is the first principles of philosophy, the root and ground of all philosophy, the several books of the Bible will be noticed in a philosophical light. The book of Job is perfectly philosophical in its principles, whether it be fact or fiction, but I will treat it as I believe it to be, a literal fact, because the narrative shows one great overruling power, infinite in knowledge as well as power; and also a secondary power, the source of wrong, but entirely subject to the greater power. It shows that man is an instrumentality in the hand of and at the disposal of the greater power to accomplish wise and necessary purposes. It also proves the warfare for which man was created, and shows that affliction is needful, and that if the soldier of the cross is called to bear the affliction the rewerd is greater than the affliction. It also shows that the great Almighty can support men to endure anything that is needful to be endured, and he does not do work that is not necessary. Job is richer in example than in type, but it is a type also, for it shows clearly what may occur to holy men and women in the gospel age of the world. The afflicted Christian with clear conscience may see in Job that the Lord rules, and all will be right in the end. Job proves that man may be perfect in this life, and it is not for reward, but for principle. It is the choice of the changed heart. It shows further that the Lord may take men through the most bitter experience, and that they will afterwards rejoice at the results of their experience. It may fall on those that are righteous in the sight of the Lord, but it will work out for them a far more exceeding and eternal weight of glory. This narrative shows that true, spiritual Christians may so study the Lord and His nature, and His will, and His manner of dealing with men, that they may see and know, and say things that will surprise and alarm the unthinking people around them, Job ix:24 and various other places, but they will be right in the sight of the Lord. The book of Job teaches that the Lord can sustain us under the most bitter circumstances that is possible to man, and is a written letter to every perfect-hearted man or woman, and it is from the Lord. Let the fire be hot as it may be (for surely Job's furnace was hot as was the furnace into which the Hebrews were cast at Babylon), He that calls them is with them, let them hold fast and conquer. This furnace of affliction, and the fiery furnace, have no doubt sustained millions under the sharpest trials, both in literal and figurative fire.

The book of Job is a signal reproof to all the earth that does not know the Lord, for Job had studied the Lord correctly before Revelation was written. The law of nature is sufficient to lead the mind to the author of nature, and obtain divine acceptance. The laws of nature govern the universe, but are under the direct control of its author to carry out his purposes of wisdom in all nature. Revelation is an additional favor for which those that have it are very responsible for the improvement of so great an advantage. But the main design reaches far beyond the mere interest of the human race; its duration and usefulness are of endless design. The human race is the instrumentality through and by which this revelation is made, and to make revelation is one of the principal designs for the creation and existence of man. The faithful may trust in any affliction, and the faithful trust will be supported. Our Lord and captain and commander and our leader in the great spiritual warfare, suffered trouble, affliction, persecution and death, at the hands of his enemies. It required him to do so to be a conquerer, and the same is required of all his fellow soldiers if they prove conquerers. Let them trust, the reward is sure. From the third to the thirteenth chapter there are two features worthy of special notice: First, the language of Job exhibits a highly cultivated mind, a wise and thoughtful improvement in and of his life, and a vast power of intellect. His language was the language of desperation. His words struck with terror and awful weight, and utterly confounded those that came to try to comfort him. But he still held fast with unshaken confidence to his Lord. The other thought is that men may be overzealous in a mistaken cause and under wrong impressions, and may say many things out of place, and suppose they are right when they are wrong. We may also learn from Job what are the conditions of a true, reliable faith, for he held fast to his integrity or confidence in the Lord when he was under the sharpest trials that ever fell on flesh and blood, so far as we have any record. In the thirty-first chapter his words show the condition on which his faith was perfectly immoveable. The ground of human faith and hope is in the Lord, but the condition of faith living and growing so as to become perfect and imperishable is in the agent, or in the man. For when a man or woman studies, learns, and sees that the Lord loves, reproves and saves those that keep a pure heart and life, and a clear conscience, and can stand before the searcher of hearts and lay claim to a perfect and blameless life and heart, then such faith cannot be moved, and that we see in the thirty-first chapter of Job. In the first twelve verses he treats of purity of heart and life and a clear conscience, and says if he is not clear let judgment fall on him. From the thirteenth to the twenty-second verse he makes his servants and the poor equal with himself, and called for a curse to fall upon him if he failed in this.

From the twenty-fourth to the twenty-eighth verse he protests against idolatry, submits the guilty to punishment, and then says he has not returned evil to his enemies, that he had cared for the stranger and that he had not covered his transgressions. He also said that he had not feared the contempt of the multitude, or of families to keep silence in the presence of wrong, and then appeals to the Almighty, and to his enemies, and declares that he obtained his land honestly. "If not," he says, "let it bring forth thistles and cockles instead of wheat and barley."

A faith that is held on such conditions cannot fail, and will never deceive its possessor, and it did not deceive Job, for as the Lord approved Job at the first, so he approved him at the last, and blessed him more than before his sore affliction. But as the book of Job has been considered as a logical teacher, another thought will be in place. That is that the three men who first came to comfort him were so astonished that they sat down with him upon the ground seven days and seven nights and none spoke a word to him.

After all this time he broke the silence and cursed his day. By this time these men recovered from their astonishment so far as to venture to reply to him, but how they wronged him in their three replies apiece. But he stood in the divine presence and did not fear or blush to declare that his life was righteous. During all this Elihu was a spectator, and was wrathy at the three men because they had condemned Job, but had not answered his arguments. Then he spoke very confidently of himself that he would show Job wisdom, and spoke with great boldness and at some length. But what did the Lord say to the self-important Elihu? He said, "Who is this that darkeneth counsel by words without knowledge?" Do not these narratives exhibit self-important, conceited human nature? But after the ends of wisdom were accomplished by Job's affliction, then the Lord approves him, and condemned the three that had condemned Job, and conferred a name on him quite above the name and memory of the greater part of the great men of the earth, as well as long life and much wealth. Surely there would have been a want in revelation if the book of Job was not in it. Surely the book of Job is a logical teacher and the Bible could not be complete without it.

In the first chapter of Job, verse 11, Satan answered the Lord and said, "But put forth thine hand now, and touch all that he hath and he will curse thee to thy face. And the Lord said unto Satan, behold all that he hath is in thy power, only upon himself put not forth thine hand." And Satan sent the heathen to take away the oxen, and the asses and to slay the servant.

He caused fire to fall and consume the sheep and the servants who kept them, and sent other heathen to take away the camels and to slay the servants that kept them. He employed the wind to destroy the house in which Job's ten children were feasting, and they were dead. But in that fight Satan was overcome by Job. In Job ii:5 Satan challenges for another fight with Job if he could afflict his person. But the Lord said, "Behold he is in thine hand, but save his life." Immediately Job was smitten with sore boils from head to foot, and that was not all, for his wife said to him, "Curse God and die." But the affliction did not stop here, for the three professed friends of Job agreed to meet Job at the same time to comfort him, but their comfort proved to be the most severe abuse. Still there was more to come for Elihu came up with the highest boast that ever a man made, but his comfort was no better than that of the other three.

Did not the Lord give him the sharpest rebuke that ever was given to a man? Chapter xxxviii, 2. But why would the Lord give Satan power over the best man in all the earth? How can theology and philosophy marry at this point? A little correct thought will make both perfect in the narrative given of Job.

If Job had not been given into the hand of Satan Job could not have overcome him. Again, when Satan gave the challenge to fight with Job, if the Lord had not suffered them to meet and fight, then there would have been an excuse in the mouth of Satan even at the judgment, and ever after, that his opportunities to gain and hold the world had not been perfect. But when he got all he asked for, or could hope for, and was so perfectly overcome, then Job's part of the warfare was perfect.

It was a real necessity that such a victory should be gained over Satan's power then and there, and Job was the highly honored person that was appointed to make that signal display. As this world and the human race have their existence expressly for the warfare, they will certainly make it perfect. Hence it need not be thought strange concerning the fiery trial which is to try the soldier of the cross, but rather think it the precise object for which they live to meet and fight, and overcome the enemy of the cross. When Satan sees the steadfast servant of Christ, faithful and true in all points of duty and of conscience, and throws out his challenge, neither the soldier of the cross nor his Lord can offord to let this challenge pass, but the soldier must meet and fight and overcome whatever enemy is brought before him. Was not this warfare inaugurated by the ordaining of Jesus Christ, the mediator and the atoner and the reigning Sovereign of the earth, and the Creator, who suffered the world to be given into the hands of the wicked that the wicked might be overcome by their own works? Hence those that voluntarily choose the wrong are led by its champion, but that entire element must be overcome by the soldier of the cross, and that must be done in every age of the world. Hence if none but Job was found in the earth to stand perfectly in the cause of right, then Job alone overcame in and for the age in which he lived. And if there were seven thousand to stand with the prophet Elijah, these overcame all the rest of the world that did not act with them in the Baal idolatry. The most terrible afflictions generally fall on the most sanctified lives. Is not this all the reason why the narrative of Job is found in the Bible? And is not the reason an all-sufficient one?

PSALMS.

The book of Psalms contains an immeasurable amount of instruction of exceeding great value. Many of the Psalms describe the life of Christ in this world, each in its own way; and also his death, his humility, how he was persecuted, and as a man of fervent prayer, returning good for evil. They also tell of hi submission to all the abuses of the people for whom he came to die. The Psalms contain the most exalted examples of thanksgiving and of praise, and show so many reasons why men should praise the Lord for his wonderful works to the children of men, for his mighty acts, for his boundless mercy, for subduing the enemies of the righteous, for the reliability of his word, and for the abundance of his promises, giving comfort, peace and joy. The Psalms are an exhaustless fountain of excellency, greatness, wisdom, and comfort. In them the heart can find a sovereign balm for every wound, a cordial for every fear. No one can estimate the worth of the Psalms.

Proverbs and Ecclesiastics. These writings of Solomon have several advantages that some other writings have not. Solomon was naturally wise, and he was endowed with superior wisdom because he asked the Lord for it of choice rather than for riches or long life. Added to that he was favored with the spirit of inspiration, and probably had the largest experience of any one up to his day, and equal to any since his day. Thus he was prepared in the providence of the Lord to do the work the Lord designed that he should do, to contribute his part in making perfect the Lord's revelation and to give the world and the church these very important parts of the scripture.

These writings of Solomon are a mine of wisdom

and knowledge. They are also a mint of value infinitely more precious than gold. They show the road to a life of purity, and they are a lamp and light to enable us to shun the road to corruption and death. There is found the contrast between virtue and vice, right and wrong, wisdom and folly, and these instructions for old and young, for ruler and subject, for parents and children, for husband and wife, and for all conditions in life.

The song of Solomon contains figurative expressions, showing the love that our Lord entertains for the true spiritual church that he bought with His own blood, and that he holds to be His own bride. It also shows the love that the true spiritual church entertains for their Lord that redeemed and saved them, in whose hearts the kingdom is set up, Luke xvii:21. These are given under the type and figure of the highest ecstasy of the marriage relation, and make a revelation of the love of Christ to the church, and the church to Christ that is not made elsewhere. It is not adapted to, or designed for a free and indiscriminate use in public. It is for the rational, honest thinking Christian, and especially those that live in marriage relation, and that appreciate and love as that relation was designed, and as the very word implies. All truly loyal companions in marriage can appreciate the song of Solomon, and see the depth of idea that these expressions convey in regard to the love that our Lord bears to His church and people. So the Lord makes a perfect revelation of Himself in these particulars. When the song of Solomon is regarded in the light of reason all must see that these parts of Scripture could not be omitted without leaving the Scripture imperfect. This is true because the marriage relation was ordained and held so sacred expressly to teach the human race, and especially the church, all the relations the church and the world sustained to their Creator, but in particular, the relation the spiritual and true worshippers sustain to the bridegroom who bought them and made them His bride.

Now this part of the book of Revelation that employs for its figures the highest esctasy of the marriage relation, fails to show the slightest hint of plurality in companionship, but in every expression the language conveys the idea of one. All the writing of Solomon, if rationally considered, will prove the nature of His errand into this world; and a very conspicuous part of that was to definitely settle, and to show on logical ground, the true nature and design of marriage. The fact that he had taken to himself, according to the laws that then existed, one thousand women, together with all his superior advantages, would make him, of all men most fit to speak on the question of marriage and the relation of the sexes. And besides what he says in the song he speaks with a certain voice in both his other writings. In Proverbs chap. 5, vers. 15 to 19: "Let thy fountain be blessed, and rejoice with the wife of thy youth." Eighteenth: "Let her be as the loving hind and the pleasant roe; let her breasts satisfy thee at all times, and be thou ravished always with her love." Thus the man is directed to make one only his companion, and give one wife the affection of his heart. But there is also an admonition to let her be his own, and not a stranger's with him. And it is set forth in the clearest manner that the marriage relation shall not be infringed, neither on the part of the husband nor the wife, in no way embracing all the pretentions of the medical profession, including obstetrics. Proverbs, chap. 6, vers. 27, 28, 29. The 27th verse reads, "Can a man take fire in his bosom and his clothes not be burned up?" Verse 28th: "Can one go upon hot coals and his feet not be burned?" The questions are their own answers and the strongest figures in nature.

The 29th verse contains two clauses, very short. The first does not show the sense of the passage, but clearly defines the criminality of what is said in the last clause, but the last clause shows the sense of the three verses and gives a clear definitation of what is forbidden in the passage.

The verse reads, "So he that goeth in to his neighbor's wife, whosoever toucheth her shall not be innocent." Touching the neighbor's wife even professionally, so called, is adultery in the light of this passage.

These passages secure the right of man or woman to have their companion exclusively without violation by any living, but if the rule is violated it is adultery as naturally as that fire will burn. Men and women have equal rights in the relation. There is no polygamy lawful to either man or woman. The same sentiment is reiterated in Ecclesiastics ix: 9. It reads "Live joyfully with the wife whom thou lovest." If there is more than one none can be loved.

I have noticed such parts of the scriptures as my purpose required, to maintain the clearest philosophy of the scripture. It has been seen that the atonement was the starting point of all nature, and necessarily must precede all things, and that by him, the atoner, were all things created that are in heaven, and that are in the earth, visible or invisible, whether they be thrones or dominions or principalities or powers. All things were created by and for him. And He is before all things and by him all things consist.

As the prophecies come next under consideration, it is naturally supposable that the atonement and atoner would be a conspicuous part of prophecy.

Let us commence with the book of Isaiah, which is a peculiar part of the inspired volume. Notice his bold manner of speaking of things in the future. his very plain predictions and descriptions. When the fulfillment occurs it is and has been so plain that the prophecy cannot fail to be remembered. Among these bright prophecies the leading thought is the Messiah—his kingdom and everlasting reign, his life, his death and his final victory. These are all seen in many of the chapters. Chapter ii:1-5; iv and vii: 10-16; ix:6-11; xi:1-12; xii and xxiii:16-18; xxxii: 1-8; xxxv and xl:1-12; xlix from first to middle; li, li, lii, liii, lv:1.7; lix:16-20; lx, lxi, lxii and lxiii. There is much more, but not so plain to the unthinking mind. But with all these very plain prophecies very plainly spoken seven or eight hundred years before they came to pass, still there are persons to dispute their truth.

There is no discord or lack of harmony in any of it, but it is philosophical when the propecy came to pass so clearly that common sense cannot evade the fact that events which are seen are the fulfillment of certain prophecies, and surely the atonement and the atoner are the great source and central thought of the book of Isaiah.

The peophecy of Jeremiah contains instructions of highest importance, and worthy of the most minute consideration, because the highest use of the record is to instruct on certain points not readily seen without the closest attention, such as the spiritually adulterous character of the Jews, and how far they had forsaken the Lord's pure ways, and still counted themselves righteous, and showing also how narrow is the Christian's path. They were the type of the church under Christ, and also a most signal warning not to be led or influenced by a ministry that does not follow Christ. So completely were the false prophets disguised that Jeremiah, the true prophet, of the Lord, thought they were true prophets and charged the Lord with greatly deceiving Jerusalem and the people, because the thing that these prophets had said had not come to pass. See chapter four, verse ten, where the prophet said, "Ah, Lord God, surely thou hast greatly deceived this people and Jerusalem saying, ye shall have peace, whereas the sword reacheth unto the soul." So completely were these pretending prophets disguised that even the truely called and chosen servant of the Lord was confounded when the word that they spoke professedly in the name of the Lord was not fulfilled. The type is seen in the professed ministers of Christ to-day, who come not as the self-denying soldiers and followers of him that suffered and died for the truth's sake, to endure hardness as did their Lord. But they aim to lord it over God's heritage, and if they do not succeed in that, they are not a success.

But the type shows where these preachers originated, that nearly fills the Christian church, but do not reform the church or the world. They are defined in chapter xiv and 14th verse, in these words: "Then the Lord said unto me, the prophets prophesy lies in my name; I sent them not, neither have I commanded them, neither spake I unto them. They prophesy unto you a false vision and divination, a thing of naught, and the deceit of their heart." Now, if the prophet Jeremiah was so deceived, what might we think of the professed lights of the world to-day? Is it too much for every man and woman that has hope in the Lord to search for themselves until they really see and know the true path of right in the light of the word of the Lord? But the minister that the Lord calls and sends to-day as He called and sent Jeremiah twenty-four hundred years ago, will find when he would preach the most needful truths a large element in the visible church that will hate and persecute him and often would, if they could, have him put to death. The self-commissioned minister speaks to them smooth things, and it is much more pleasing to the unrenewed heart than the truth. The Lord's ministers are in the war, it is their very business to be there, and if they are true soldiers they will, like their Lord, find enemies till their struggle is ended by death. If it is not lawful for their enemies to put them to death, then they will crucify them in their usefulness, or in their good name, or put them down some way, but put them down. These servants of the cross can read

Jeremiah and see that the Lord has promised them that kind of a life, by the record of what the Lord's prophets suffered at the hands of the wicked for the truth's sake, and they will take courage and go on. One very striking feature of Jeremiah is that the Lord sent by Jeremiah, offering the people pardon and protection if they would turn from their wickedness, aggravated as their sins were described to be; but they treated him with disdain and derision and continued to treat His messengers so until the enemy came and carried them away, according to the word of Jeremiah from the Lord. These types pointed to the Christian era, and make revelation perfect at a point where nothing else does.

The idea has been advanced that the captivity was the clearest type of a backslider from a sanctified life. But their return to the land was the type of a sanctified life and was a promise, by type, to those that have gone back from a sanctified life, yet still love the cause, and do not deny that love, but repent as sincerely as the Jews did, that they may return to that peace from which they fell, though their temple will not be to them so grand. Their repentence is read in the one hundred and thirty-seventh Psalm, and in various other scriptures.

How striking is the similarity between the typical people, the Jews, and the anti-type in the Christian era! The Jews were carried captives to Babylon and remained seventy years. But the Lord prepared Cyrus to issue his proclamation to the Jews to return to Jerusalem and build the city and temple and wall, and to re-establish their religion under the divine laws, and to restore the Jews to their inheritance. After the Lord had restored them to their much desired rights and prosperity under divine protection for a time, how soon they retrograded into habits of wickedness! But the period drew near when their Deliverer should come, and He did come, but He did not suit them. As a nation they rejected Him, and the authorities bought Him from one that was willing to sell Him for thirty pieces of silver, and they crucified Him. But after all that they still claimed to be the Lord's people. Soon after that they ceased to be a people, but were scattered and driven into every nation, and they remain a typical people to this day. But when in the providence of the Lord the true spiritual church was passively brought into the moral wilderness of oppression, trouble, poverty, persecution for Christ's, and for conscience sake, they remained so for a time and times and half a time, or not far from twelve centuries. The Lord did not send Cyrus, the monarch, to rescue them, but he did send a young, single-handed priest, Martin Luther, to break the power of oppression, and to set the gospel in a much clearer light, in the sixteenth century. And in the eighteenth century he set up a government, like the republic of Israel, that acknowledged no king but the Lord, namely, the United States. Its example has weakened the power of tyranny in all nations, and it is called an asylum for the oppressed the world over.

Now we change our ruler by electing a new one, but we do not elect a new Lord, neither does he change. In view of the fact that the church, after being rescued from tyranny and put in possession of liberty and independence, has so mingled with the world as to lose her identity, and corrupted her doctrines and has become so weak as to be a prey to the infidel, is the fulfillment of these types and signs to us in the nineteenth century? Does the same God reign over us to-day that cast off the Jews into every nation? If so, are there any sign? And is that sign to us destruction? Shall we fear? But the human race was created to do what they are doing, or would any one dispute the truth of that? If so, then do you hold that the Lord has been deceived in His design or His object in bringing and keeping the race in existence? Surely not. But if so much sin should be permitted as should answer the ends of wisdom, and should remain while it is useful, and no more, then when the philosophy of this is seen, who can be certain that the ends of wisdom might not come nearly being accomplished, and if so the end draweth nigh.

Now a nation cannot rise or fall, or exist only by and under the ruling of divine providence. Most cities of the east were promised to be destroyed, and these promises have not failed. Some of these are Syria, Assyria, Babylon, Tyre, and various others, and Moab, Ethiopia, Egypt, Israel and Judah, and other countries and cities.

In the twenty-fifth chapter of Jeremiah is a promise of the destruction of all nations, commencing at the city that was called by his name. This beginning certainly has been most signally made in the city of Jerusalem. Now is all this done without an object? Can any believer so regard it? Surely not. But the nations that choose their own ways and delight in their abominations, Isaiah lxvi, 3-4, the Lord also will choose their delusions, and suffer them to practice only such as will bring about the wise and necessary ends for which the world and the race of man were created, namely, the exposition of, and the perfect conquest over sin. And as nations choose the ways of delusions, the Lord gives or rather permits them to choose such delusions as will be held on record and exhibit national sins showing their nature and their reward. And when any nation runs its wicked course as far as can be made pofitable then its destruction is at hand. Sin cannot be permitted without wisdom and necessity in permitting it. Here is reason for the rise and fall of nations, and also for

17

the destruction of all nations when they have answered the ends of wisdom in this world.

It is not for the sake of the nations that the Lord keeps them in existence. But they are needful to bring the cause of wrong where it can be overcome by the right and to make a show of it openly, triumphing over all the power of wrong.

The five chapters of Lamentations set forth the sentiment of all pure hearts when their friends are in trouble, and they are a confession of sin, and the full justifying of the Lord in national judgment.

Ezekiel prophesided near the time of Jeremiah, and the objects of both prophecies were of kindred character, both showing the people's idolatry and adultery, both spiritual and physical, and their corruption of various kinds, and inviting them to turn from their sins and find mercy. Both prophets tell the people their sinful course would end in their captivity, and Ezekiel speaks of the Christian Church in various ways. Under the figure of dry bones he shows something of the superior condition of the Lord's people after the Holy Ghost was given, and speaks of the judgment of Gog and Magog, and of the history of the temple and its appendages. Some of this is in the future, but what has past is in such complete harmony with all the rest of the Bible that we can well afford to trust for those parts that are not yet seen.

Prophecy of Daniel. In the first chapter there is a notable event; Daniel and his three friends being determined to keep themselves pure and faithful, would not eat of the king's diet lest it might defile them.

How signally the Lord helped them to carry out their purpose, and so signally distinguished them. For in the second chapter the king dreams and forgets his dream, but demands of the wise men to make known to him the dream and the interpretation. They declare that no man living can do that.

The king commands them to be put to death, but Daniel rescues them by telling the king his dream and the interpretations, and when this was done that monarch of the earth fell down on his face before Daniel and worshiped him, the Hebrew captive. Was ever such a change heard of before or since? What a revelation it makes of the Lord of how he rewards his perfect, faithful followers or servants, and how it shows what absolute power the Lord has over all men good and bad.

In chapter third the king set up a golden image and commanded all people to fall down and worship it, and if they would not they should be cast into the fiery furnace. But these men, Daniel's friends, refused to worship the image. Then the king in his wrath ordered the furnace to be made hotter than was needful for common use, and at this extra degree of heat these men were cast into the burning furnace bound with all their clothing. But the king beheld four men walking in the fire without hurt, and when he called them his three captives came out without hurt on either person or clothing. Never was there any person so distinguished as these three that had been faithful even in the midst of opposing powers. What revelation was made by this transaction to that heathen people, and no less to all people to whom it has come since, or ever will come.

In the fourth chapter the same king dreams again and sees a great tree and it was cut down, but was to live again (verse 17) "to the intent that the living may know that the most high ruleth in the kingdoms of men, and giveth it to whomsoever he will, and sitteth up over it the basest of men." But Daniel must show the interpretation for the others could not. Daniel told the king that he should be driven from men, and dwell with the beasts, and eat of their food and be wet with the dew of heaven for seven years, all of which was done. But the king did again resume his throne after all this was fulfilled.

The fifth chapter treats of a successor, Belshazzar, and he makes a feast in his pride and wickedness, and the most wicked act of the feast was to bring the sacred vessels of the Lord's temple and defile them.

While this wicked act was being done there appeared the fingers of a man's hand, and wrote on the wall. The king saw the part of the hand that wrote and the writing, but could not read it, and was alarmed. But who could read and interpert the mysterious writing? All the wise men tried, but all failed, but Daniel was found and read the writing and told the meaning to the king that morally he lacked weight and politically his kingdom was removed from him, all of which was fulfilled in that self-same night. The true God was again revealed to the heathen, and his servant Daniel was again signally distinguished.

In the sixth chapter the king made Daniel ruler next to himself. But it displeased the natives to see the captive above them and they obtained a decree from the king that if any person would pray or ask petition of any being except the king, for thirty days that they should be cast into the den of lions. They did this because they had noticed Daniel's unwavering fidelity to his God and hoped they could find him praying. They found him prompt to the hour. Daniel did, with windows open, kneel and pray three times a day as before. Then they brought the case before the king that Daniel had violated the king's decree, and they claimed that the penalty should be fulfilled, and Daniel was cast into the den of lions and was there one night. But in early morning the king was at the den, and called to Daniel and he answered, and the king commanded Daniel to be taken out of the den, and that his accusers should be thrown into the den but the beasts devoured them.

Now how vastly these narratives enrich revelation! They show how the Lord rewards the pure, and the holy, and how he delivers his faithful servant, and does honor them that in the singleness of their hearts do honor him. Another lesson that is typically taught in these narratives is that the Christian's deliverance is sure.

The first chapter shows how the providence is exercised toward Christians who are determined to live pure in the midst of impurity. Revelation could not be perfect without it. In the case of the first dream the king commanded an impossibility in the light of human power and wisdom. When these circumstances surround the Christian, which they often do essentially but not literally, this narrative proves that God is there and that the Christian was brought there on purpose to meet and overcome that difficulty and overcome it in the name of the Lord. In these revelations are seen philosophy, cause and effect, and the revelation is to all people. believer and unbeliever, Christian or infidel.

In the third chapter touching the deliverance from the fire of the furnace, how many millions of Christians when in the furnace of tribulation or affliction have seen their promise of help in that very narrative, and have received deliverance from the same source.

The fourth chapter shows us the same result of becoming proud and self-exalted. Who can estimate the value of that narrative?

The fifth chapter has more in it than is visible, for in it we see that when one becomes proud, and so regardless and impudently wicked that he will desecrate and defile the sacred vessels of the Lord's temple, that he is ripe for perdition any hour. But what is meant by these vessels that were the object of the Lord's care, and that so soon called down his judgment on Belshazzar who had dared to desecrate them? Those vessels of the Lord's temple were the type of the Lord's people. Each vessel was the type of one person. Every sane minded person has the agency over one of these precious vessels, that is himself, for the intellect and the human heart, the seat of affection, are more precious material than the gold of which those vessels of the temple were made, as well as the conscience and the will and the entire physical structure. Whoever will defile and willingly desecrate the spiritual vessel is near the road to perdition.

The lesson of the sixth chapter, Daniel among the lions, was to reveal the Lord as one every where present to help whenever needful. How many millions of Christians have been passively thrown among the fierce and powerful enemy that would devour them if they could, but have been as signally brought from among them without hurt as Daniel was. How could any of the book of Daniel be spared? The prophecy of Daniel contains much more that is very worthy of notice, and enters most fully into the harmonious and vast design of the whole scripture.

The spiritual kingdom of Christ is here brought to view, and the interpretation given and published.

In chapter eight is another vision of another kind which was also interpreted and published.

In the ninth chapter Daniel seeks mercy of the Lord by prayer and fasting, sackcloth and ashes, which is humiliation. He seeks mercy for his people confessing "our sins," not "your sins." He said, "We have sinned," not "the people have sinned," but confessed the Lord was holy, just and good in all the afflictions of the Jews. From the sixteenth to the nineteenth verses Daniel prays for the pardon of his people, and while he was thus in prayer the man Gabriel was caused to fly swiftly and touch him. Here Daniel's importance was again brought to view, and he was informed when that vast work, Daniel ix:24, should be accomplished.

The tenth, eleventh and twelfth chapters of Daniel show other revelations made to him running until the close of time, or till the end be.

Hosea, Joel, Amos and Micah, all four prophesied near the time that Isaiah did, shortly before Israel was removed from being a people, and taken into Assyrian captivity, or it seems more like hopeless exile, with their inheritance and their nationality lost because of their sinful course in life. These prophets all except Joel reproved both Israel and Judah for their sins and admonished them from the Lord that if they would forsake their sinful ways and return to the Lord he would receive and be merciful to them. But they disbelieved them, and abused and perscuted them, but they found the ruin of which they had been warned did come upon them. This is a type of those that sin carelessly or willfully after receiving the knowledge of the truth, or of the backslider from a sanctified life. For the Israelites inherited a land that was the type of heaven, as respects the Lord's favor and protection and of victory over all that oppose them and of enjoyment. But with all their light and their favors from the Lord they made and worshiped idols and denied their true God. For this they were cast away. The lesson that as a type it teaches to Christians is that there is not only a possibility, but there is danger of falling into sin and being lost, even from the sanctified life.

Another feature of most of these prophets is that passages are found in them that plainly bring the atonement to view, and the church under Christ in some of its characteristics or distinguishing features, showing the atonement to be a prominent feature of almost every department of scripture, as surely it should be. Joel speaks of the pouring out of the spirit so plainly that the language cannot be mistaken although uttered more than seven hundred years before it occured. Jeremiah and Ezekiel prophesied shortly before, but some part of their prophecies were fulfilled after Judah was carried captive to Babylon.

Habakkuk and Yephaniah were near the same time. By these prophets the Lord plead with Judah to reform their ways, to quit their idolatry and return to their Lord, and told them the consequence of disobedience, which would be the sacrifice of their land. Their city and temple and all that they loved would be given into the hands of their enemies, the heathen. But like Israel they would not harken, but persecuted the Lord's messengers until their cause was hopeless and the Lord gave them into the hands of the king of Babylon. Now here is the backslider from the sanctified life, but who repents before the Lord, and confesses his sins to the Lord (not to man only as the sins were against men) but seeks pardon of the Lord, like Judah when their repentance moved the Lord's pity for them to reinstate them. When Judah was restored to their own land it teaches that Christians may be restored in a very similar manner, when they repent and seek with all the heart and all its depths. The building of the temple and the wall is to the Christian the revival of practice and doctrine of the Christian life, or if considered collectively it means revival in the church.

The prophecy of Jonah was likely the earliest of the smaller prophets. There have been those who boast of their knowledge of philosophy, but question them but a little beyond their sight, and their cause and effect will be a perfect failure, and they cannot believe Jonah for want of philosophy. But when God is demonstrated in nature without the Bible then there is no impossibility, and when that God saw it was a stern necessity to make such a revelation of himself as is made in and by the narrative of Jonah, then where is the lack of philosophy? O, shame! It is said his words shall not pass away, but why not?

The Lord brought this little planet and the human race into existence to make a revelation of himself by which all his subjects may know him in all the endless future, and also to reveal and conquer all his enemies. And now what if the great Supreme was willing to reveal himself up to the full extent that the narrative reveals him, that all his subjects in all the endless future might read and know who and what he is in these respects, the wisdom and goodness in ruling, but the certainty of being obeyed? Now whether these remarks are the best solution of Jonah or not it is plainly philosophical and scriptural, and if any one cannot improve it let him not dispute it. The Bible could not be complete without it.

OBADIAH AND HAGGAI.

Obadiah treats of the destruction of Edom, which prophecy has long since been fulfilled.

Nahum treats of the destruction of Nineveh fulfilled long ago.

Haggai contains two chapters, and their importance cannot be too highly estimated. It shows us what attention the Lord's work claims at the hands of the church. No personal interest should be thought of when the special work of the Lord demands the time of his people, their interest or their heart; and herein we see why prosperity does not crown our labors, and why the Lord reproves us in the failure of our crops, our wages and our comforts. The promises to the Jews of prosperity in the performance of their work and duties are a type and a promise to the true spiritual servant of Christ when the Lord sends him to build up his spiritual house, or its defenses (true Bible doctrine.) If such a one find opposition, Haggai is a plain teacher to him, showing the road to success. These two chapters of Haggai could not be spared from the Bible.

Zachariah, fourteen chapters, at the same time with Haggai, also treats of building the temple or house of the Lord at Jerusalem. But the most conspicuous features of Zachariah are the atonement and the atoner, and the spiritual church under them.

How philosophical is this entire department of scripture, the prophecy of Zachariah! It shows the Lord's servants at work in opposition to this world, for the accomplishment of an object greater than the temperal interests of all the earth, and they finish the work,

Malachi, the latest of the prophets prophesied after the Jews returned from Babylon to inherit their land and nation. This prophecy shows how priests and people again descended into sin, but the chief item in it is the messenger of the covenant, the refiner, the Christ.

NEW TESTAMENT.

Having very briefly considered the thirty-nine books of the Old Testament, in the light of the only perfect system of philosophy in nature, I demand to know where is the lack of either harmony or philosophy in these books? And where outside of them can clear reason be found for anything we see that will not come to a question which cannot find a philosophical answer?

As the atonement is evidently the leading theme of the Old Testament, and the great important center of all the thoughts the Old Testament contains, and is the condition of all creature existence, then if all the prophecies concerning the atonement is fulfilled in the person of some one, is it not proven that such person was the Messiah if revelation be in perfect harmony with reason. and reason cannot be found apart from revelation then the slander that says the scriptures cannot be sustained by reason would be removed from the Bible and its author? The New Testament shows the fulfillment of the Old Testament and there is no book sustained by so much testimony and so many authors as the new Testament.

Take the four gospels which instruct us concerning the physical origin of Christ, its author. He was the son of a woman but not of a man. He was the son of God as really as any man is the son of some man. The law consecrated men to the office of priest at the age of thirty years, but when, where and how did our Lord fulfill this law of consecration that he might lawfully act in the temple? We are not left without certainty on this subject, for Mathew xxi:25, and Mark xi:30 and Luke xx:4, all record the answer to that question as to where he received authority to act in the temple, and who gave him such authority.

All three, Matthew, Mark and Luke, tell us that He referred them to the baptism of John for all the answer He gave them. The law to consecrate a priest required to wash him with water, Exodus xxiv:4, at the door of the tabernacle of the congregation; also Leviticus viii:6, with water, at the door, verse 3.

But our Lord received His washing by His baptism,

at the door, or the opening act of His endless rule or reign, which commenced by His baptism, filling the law of consceration. This was the door of Christ's authority, or His public action. But the anointing oil and the blood of the altar were sprinkled on them that were consecrated, and on all their garments. That was the type of, and was fulfilled when the spirit, like a dove, did light on Jesus after He was baptised, or washed with water, at the door or threshold of His visible authority. Then He was lawfully a priest, having fulfilled the letter of the law. After this He was tempted of the devil in the wilderness for forty days, that He might succor those who are tempted. After He returned, the evidences of His divine character were brighter and plainer than before. A person who can cleanse the leprosy by his word is divine. The very use of leprosy is to illustrate sin. The poison spreads irresistably and hopelessly, but this man of Nazareth said, "Be thou clean; and the leprósy was cleansed." The blind of this world cannot be cured by human skill, but Jesus, by the word of His power, caused the blind to see. This is the only figure of spiritual blindness, and it is the only true figure of spiritual healing, and is an infallible proof of divine power. Furthermore, the deaf and dumb, physically, are the only figures of the spiritually deaf and dumb, and there was no remedy in human power to relieve from their misfortune. But the author of the New Testament did cause the deaf to hear and the dumb to talk. Is it not God that can do this? Another evidence of His divinity or Godhead is that He raised the dead to life physically, and when He said "Thy sins be forgiven thee," that was a positive pledge to the whole earth that He could and would raise the spiritually dead to life. God alone can give life to the dead. Another indubitable testimony of His Messiahship was that He cast out devils. This was done before the physical senses of spectators, insomuch that none seemed to have denied the fact. This also can be done by divine power only. Now, as the leprosy, deafness, blindness and deadness are the fruits of the enemy and fallen nature, and the very use of all these is to reveal to the world the true condition of the unrenewed nature of man, and as the physical is the only type of the spiritual, then the personage that has demonstrated His power so fully to subdue and to master and to conquer by His word, all of these, most undoubtedly, demonstrates Himself to be God. He healed a nobleman's son, passed unseen through the multitude, gave a miraculous draught of fishes, cured a demoniac, healed Peter's wife's mother, healed a paralytic, cured an impotent man, restored a withered hand, healed the centurion's servant, stilled the tempest, healed the woman of her twelve years' weakness, raised Jarious' daughter, gave miraculous power to the apostles, fed five thousand on nearly nothing, walked on the sea, obtained money from a fish, healed a woman of eighteen years' infirmity, cured the dropsy, withered the barren fig tree and healed the ear of Malchus. What more could be added to prove the Messiahship of the despised Nazarene, that those who trust him should not question the promises that He has made to His followers? These healings are all promises of spiritual healing.

Another class of testimony is that His life and works, words and death so influenced the whole world that by universal consent the count of time is changed. For the first four thousand years of the world were counted from the life of the first man, but from the advent of this Man the numbering of years commenced again at one.

Another class of evidence is that no person has ever lived on this earth whose life has borne any equal comparison to His in regard to the number of persons that have acknowledged and admired, and published His history. No name has been so generally and so reliably published as that of the Man of Calvary. All the New Testament writers were eye and ear witnesses. There is a book written by Prof. C. E. Stowe entitled, "Origin and History of the Books of the Bible." In that work we find a great number of authors other than the New Testament writers, who bear testimony to the person of Jesus Christ and His works as written in the New Testament. Beginning with those of the first century he gives Barnabas, Clement, Josephus, Papias, and Ignatius, five beside the sacred writers in the first century of the Christian era. In the second century there were many more. Mr. Stowe names twenty-eight authors who wrote in the second century, all bearing witness to the New Testament and to its great Author. Of those in the third century he gives the names of fifteen who wrote in support of the truth of the New Testament and its Author. And in the fourth century there are twenty-five others who are named as writers that bear witness to the New Testament truths.

In the fifth century the names of five more occur who bear testimony to the great light of the world.

Of those in the sixth century he gives the names of four more. Here is a succession of authors from the eye and ear witnesses of Christ, the author of the New Testament and his works to the present day. These are the watchmen on Zion's walls that see eye to eye.

The first stand until they see others come and talk with them, and they see and talk with others their successors, and so it is handed from hand to hand from the great author of the scripture to the present day. Now if any one will not believe in the atonement, why will he not? Surely not for want of the clearest testimony.

Another positive evidence of his Messiahship was that his teaching was pure and perfect and very plain and very offensive to the authorities, altogether unlike human nature, for the plain truth that must be told and shown condemned the authorties and caused them to seek his life, and at the right time he suffered them to take his life, for, for that cause came he to that hour.

The standard of truth and propriety that our Lord taught was, "Be ye perfect, even as your father which is in heaven is perfect." The same to the letter that is taught in the types, and there is no lower standard of acceptable life taught in the Bible anywhere.

When the time drew near that he should be offered he told his followers that such a thing should befall him, but when the reality came to pass his disciples would have defended him with the sword. But he said, "Put up your sword, for if I ask my father he would send me more than twelve legions of angels." But how then should the scriptures be fulfilled that thus it must be? And he said, "The cup that my father gave me, shall I not drink it?". These expressions show that these things were appointed to him before the world was.

In the face of this testimony, sufficient to prove

the atonement and the character of the person that made it, if anything can be proven and settled by history, then the atonement and the atoner are settled beyond a doubt.

The ground taken in these pages is to the effect that infinite wisdom created and upholds this earth and its inhabitants for some useful end or design which is not so dark but that the human mind can search it out, and see in the light of reason that this planet is the theater of war, and the human race are the soldiers. It was the essential object of their existence.

By the wars of the world we see that discipline is a necessity in war, and surely it is plain that from the calling of Abraham until the ministry of Christ, the business of the world was to make and record discipline, and to instruct the spiritual army in all its special points of power.

This army must be instructed that carnal weapons whose success is but flattering and short at best, could not succeed in the hands of the spiritual soldier, but that spiritual weapons wisely handled are reliable and no others, that right must conquer wrong, and love conquer malice, and good conquer evil, and prayers be given for curses. These are the weapons of spiritual warfare, and from the time that our Lord commenced his ministry, after his initiation to the priesthood at Jordan, the hand to hand fight commenced. The great captain of the spiritual army was the first victim, but was he conquered? Verily no, but the act of crucifying him was a necessity that he might by that appointed means become the mighty conquerer of the great enemy of the universe. But he calls men and women to the vastly high relation of being soldiers with him, and millions of them have conquered like their Master in the death of a martyr.

When the Lord stood a criminal and his friend with his sword smote off the ear of one of his enemies he bid Peter put up the carnal weapon, for he had help enough for the asking for it, "but how then should the scripture be fulfilled that thus it must be?" And with his dying breath he prayed, "Father, forgive them, they know not what they do." O, man or woman, how can you aspire so high in any other way, as to join the cause of right under the leadership of our Lord, and fight with him as he commands? If he sees good to give or honor us with the martyr's death let it be the highest exultation.

The four gospels furnish the clearest and fullest account of the fulfillment of most of the prophecies, and most of the types of the Old Testament, and furnish the most philosophical and clear testimony to the truth of the whole scripture, showing it all to be one book having but one object in view. Thus is made a grand and perfect whole of revelation showing its design and its perfection, and that it is worthy of its author, and that it is perfectly suitable in every particular for the grand and endless purpose for which it was designed.

The four Gospels show the deception and depravity of the human heart to its fullest extent, more than anything else in nature could. When the Jews looked for a Savior He came and proved himself to be the right one. But they must dictate to him what he must say and what He must do and how He must live; and when He would tell them the truth it stirred their malice, and they sought His life, and when the heathen judge or governor said, "Take ye Him and crucify Him, for I find no fault in Him," they did crucify Him. Nature knows no such thing as that except in that one case.

In the Gospels we are told by the highest authority that there will be a general judgment, when perfect justice will be meted out to all, and that the armies of the right, and also of the wrong, will be put on exhibition, which exhibition will be eternal. In the self same speech He tells us that heaven and earth shall pass away, but His words shall not pass away. Now where is the difficulty in the Scripture concerning justice or mercy or infinite goodness in any way of considering it? Here are the warning words of the infinite Lord forever held on exhibition, which were revealed to the world while it was in its probation. But it may be said those lost ones did not all of them ever see or hear those words of warning that were spoken by the divine authority personally. No, they did not; even a very great majority of the world never read or heard them read. But every responsible agent from first to last has had, or will have light equal to this in all respects essential to justice, and will be judged according to the light they have. But this revelation was made so plain and indisputable, and by the Judge in person, that no one in Christendom can fail to understand it, and all such must be affected by it. But it will bear endless testimony that the word of the Almighty itself would not be harkened to by those who chose depravity and deception. And that will prove to the heathen who are lost that the blessing of revelation to those who chose depravity would but make their condemnation the more terrible. Thus from all the earth, glory, honor, righteousness, security and indemnity will gather around the throne everlastingly.

The acts of the apostles occupy a very fitting place in making revelation perfect. Like all other Scriptures, their strength and value do not consist in knowing the secretary that their great Author employed to write them; but the important necessity for them, and the fitness they have to meet that necessity, are all sufficient proof of their divine authenticity. They are written as man does not write (see the apochryphal acts), and their teachings are not as man teaches. The Acts make perfect the points of revelation that they were designed to make, and they are not made perfect in any other way, or by any other writing. This department of scripture shows the fulfillment of the promised out pouring of the spirit of the Lord, or the Holy Ghost that was promised in many passages, and expressed in various ways and words.

Many of the types, as all the washings with water of any thing or typical cleansing with water of anything and everything that was so cleansed, all pointed to the water of life, which was the pure, cleansing instructing, life giving spirit of the Lord that should be poured out upon the world.

This was fulfilled in its fullest possible sense in the great Pentecostal outpouring. Here we are informed that the promise was fulfilled to the church, her privileges vastly extended and her purity established. Men were enabled to be fearless of the powers and authorities of the world, and to speak the boldest truths, and that to the highest authorities of the world as readily as to the low or powerless. They were willing to die for the truth if need be, or be put in prison, or be beaten with stripes, or have their goods taken from them.

All worldly things were held ready to be sacrificed for Christ and his cause. Worldly pursuits made no part of the object of their lives, but the glory of the Father, Son and Holy Ghost was their entire object, together with the salvation of the world.

The most exalted death that men could die was to be martyred for Christ's and for conscience's sake, like the martyr Stephen was, and almost all of the apostles, and a vast number of faithful ones since then. Another thing taught in the Acts is the constant warfare that goes on between right and wrong. The armies of the wrong with their carnal weapons strive to annihilate the true soldiers of the right. They do that yet and always will so far as they have power. The armies of the right with their spiritual weapons return good for evil, kindness for malice, right for wrong and with these they conquer the wrong. They always have conquered when they took the perfect weapon and used it perfectly and they always will. These spiritual weapons are the only instrumentalities by which the wrong can be conquered.

Another thing seen in the Acts is that if men think the price to high that secures the Christian's reward, they are at perfect liberty to serve the world, and stand with the opposite army for its reward, and they shall have it.

How willingly the soldiers of the cross will suffer anything or all things for their Master's sake, the loss of their goods, the hope of wealth or worldly honor, and meet their death by fire, by the cross, or be devoured by wild beasts, or be beheaded, or any other death that malice could invent, but they are victors in their death through Him that stands by them.

Another thing seen in the Acts is the Lord's care and protection over his faithful ones, as seen in the conversion of Saul of Tarsus (Paul, the apostle) for he was conscientious, and the Lord showed him that it was his privilege to suffer for the Lord, and to seek a crown that lay beyond in which many stars might glitter.

But his condition was to despise the touch of wealth, or worldly honor that would be as a cloud over his present usefulness or future prospects, or stain his conscience. We see also in the Acts that Christians may have plans, and with an honest design to serve the Lord in their plans may be like Paul who desired to go to Rome to preach the gospel, but desired a prosperous journey. But he could earn a great deal more wages for the Lord by going a perilous journey, and a perilous journey he had. Oh, how the true heart may be encouraged under the darkest clouds!

Another item is, Paul shows Christians how to finish their pilgrimage, for when he was condemned to die a martyr of the cross, he said he had fought a good fight, he had kept the faith, and he had finished his course, and he said his crown was laid up for him, that would be given to him at that day.

The twelve epistles of Paul, three of John, two of Peter, one each of James and Jude, in all twenty, and the Revelation are all in perfect harmony with all the rest of the Scripture. The New and the Old Testaments have each for its object the same thing, and both teach that the Lord had a special use for the world, and that it is accomplishing the very design for which it was created; not that any creature was put under any obligation to sin, for the promises are alike to all and the penalties are alike to all, according to their work. Thus all the world have served and ever will serve, as they themselves choose. Those that choose delusion, the Lord chooses what that delusion shall be, and overrules it; but those that choose truth, the Lord leads into the ways of truth. A perfect heart and holy life may hope in the merits of Christ for Salvation, but the careless and indifferent need not, whether in church or out of it.

The book of Revelation is more obscure in its meaning, but is not out of harmony with any other Scripture. It shows most clearly that human beings were not created for their own pleasure, nor did they incidently fall, that love and mercy might be shown in their redemption; but for reasons of stern and terrible necessity does this world of man exist. The world is filling up to the measure of its design, and there is no accident with the Lord. All men are rendering Him a service, and will everlastingly. The champion infidel who thinks he annihilates the Lord's claim to the human race, even such a man is rendering the Lord a valuable service, for He will make even the wrath of man to praise Him, and will restrain all actions and works of man that would not contribute to His praise in all His attributes.

The Darwins, Tyndalls, Huxleys, Ingersolls and who ever advocates their principles, all claim that reason is their all conquering weapon. Some of them say science, but if science does not mean reason, then it is a word without sense. They say the scripture cannot be maintained on the ground of clear logical reason, and on this ground they condemn the scripture and attempt to bring forward something for a substitute, but they make a shameful failure. But in the light of these few pages the most perfect reason, harmony and consistency are seen in the entire scripture, as well as the first and clearest principles of philosophy. Its very root is found in the Bible.

If clear reason is seen for everything in the Bible it is clear proof that it cannot be found anywhere else, and herein it is shown that Christianity can wrest the weapon from the hand of infidelity on his, the infidel's, own platform and utterly annihilate the last vestage of his argument on his own ground. Christianity shows reason in a philosophical light that cannot be moved, but the best that infidelity can do is to hold up the eternity of matter, or the late grand, high discovery, that some law of evolution has produced all creatures life. Oh, shame! But when clear, logical reason is seen for everything, and also the most indispensible necessity for everything that the Bible tells us was done, that must settle all disputes against the Bible forever.

So we close these thoughts.

A word to the reader; this short treatise on the Bible was, and is, designed to answer the infidel argument. The only argument they bring with any show of success is, that the Bible is without logic, reason, philosophy, harmony, or consistency. But if a theory is advanced that does show all these in the Bible, even if it would not be supported by the letter of the Bible, would it not answer their argument, and prove their argument to be erroneous? And does not this treatise prove that much? But if the theory cannot be condemned by the Bible, nor by anything in nature, truth, reason, or logic, then it ought not to be considered erroneous.

Does not this little book come up to such a demand as that? But if such theory is supported by Revelation, and by the book of nature, and by truth, reason, and philosophy, then is not a perfect answer to the infidel argument. And is not these pages supported by both nature and revelation? And does it not rescue the Bible and its author from the basest slander that ever was thrust at any being in the universe? Namely, the God of the Bible gave to man a revelation, but could not, did not, make it comprehensible to his capacity, or the judgment with which the Lord had endowed him. And is not the only weapon wrested from infidelity and turned against itself, as a system? And does it not annihilate the infidel argument perfectly with their own weapon on their own ground? If so, my task is done.

www.ingramcontent.com/pod-product-compliance
Lightning Source LLC
Chambersburg PA
CBHW032105220426
43664CB00008B/1136